ON THE GO

BASEBALL

MARK LITTELL

Habanero Publishing LLC

Published by:
Habanero Publishing LLC • 6040 E Montecito Ave • Scottsdale, AZ 85251

Printed in the United States of America

First Edition: 2016

ISBN 978-0-9898672-6-9 paperback

ISBN 978-0-988672-5-2 hardbound

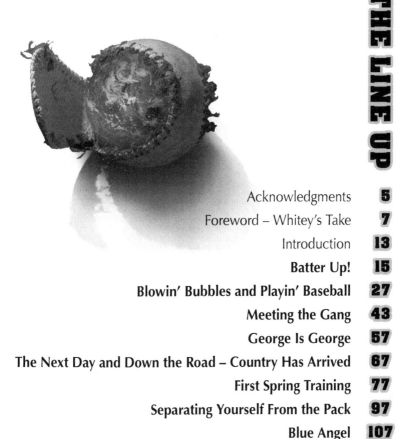

THE LINE UP

ACKNOWLEDGMENTS

Without a doubt I feel that filling up ten pages or so thanking the many folks that helped push me into writing these stories would be a bad pitch. Of the many folks who stayed after me, I give you a nod and salute for helping me start this quest and adventure into the great game of baseball.

First off Kellie Coppola, who pulled the book together, stayed after me, and did all the edits. She kept me on track. I had a conglomeration of words put down on paper told in my voice. Yeah, I'm a Country Boy but now I have advanced myself to being a cultured Country Boy. John Paul Thurau who is one of my former players also helped with a few edits and he too pushed me. Thank you, JP.

I really have to tip my hat to brother Eric who caught me and ended up on the short end of the stick many times both on and off the field. Through my first eighteen years in the Bootheel, it was an ordeal for him to just stay alive.

Craig, a businessman who has written three books himself, read a few of my stories. I wasn't trying to sell him but believe me, he is a hard sell. After reading he said, "Not many people make me laugh, but this is good. Let's see where this goes." And go it did.

My wife Sanna really pushed me to stay after it. "It will calm your soul." She's well educated and also added that I needed to learn the English language. The first time she met me she said I was "Crass." I said, "What's crass?" She told me to look it up. So much for that.

And last my German Shorthair Roscoe who is my trusty companion and always at my side really kept me in line. His vocabulary is around 200 words. On occasion he might twitch his paw then raise his head to let me know in dog telepathy, you might want to check that last sentence.

FOREWORD
WHITEY'S TAKE

first met Mark when we called him back up in '75. I had just taken over as Manager for the Royals, and had seen "Country," as he was called, pitch here and there when scouting and managing other teams. Country came up as a starter, but was more borderline and didn't fit into a starting role. In reality, the hunt for holding the lead and keeping the win in your favor had to come from the pen. We were just finding out how a set-up and closer fit into the overall scenario when going into a swing game in the late innings. A "swing game" is decided by two runs or less. In '76 we had a legitimate chance to compete and kick the Oakland A's from landing on top as they had previously proven. In the first two games of the season
I didn't know which direction to go with. I finally decided to send this cock-eyed, half-witted idiot between the lines to salvage a game. *Let's just see what Country Boy can do when under fire.*

Well, I'll be damned. He responded with 4.1 innings against Baltimore and hung onto a 1-run lead to give us a win on the third game of the season. He was pretty much a two-pitch pitcher at the time, but he seemed to want the ball in those tight spots. When he spotted up the fastball and threw that late breaking, nasty slider, he was deadly. His change-up was pretty much a void. Bonafide closer material!

When I really found out what he was like, I gave him the name "Airhead." Just point him to the mound and roll the dice. Air could get testy at times— coming into the ninth he just might walk a couple of hitters then strike out the next three. He sold a lotta beer keepin' those Kansas City fans on the edge of their seats.

One thing that was a real sight to see was when he was brought into the game to shut the door. He'd be joggin' to the mound while the speakers would be blasting away to John Denver's song "Thank God I'm A Country Boy." You bet, those fans were rockin' and rollin' when Air came in to warm up. Eventually they settled down when the hitter stepped into the box and Air did his thing. He was on in '76 and this would be Kansas City's first time to go into the ALCS (American League Championship Series).

I grew up 175 miles to the north of where Mark grew up, and on the other side of the Mississippi River. Since we were from the same neck of the woods, I knew he liked to hunt and fish. So we'd go out on occasion and knock a few birds down or drag in a few bass or trout. I'm surprised after getting to know him that he didn't bring out a half a stick of dynamite packed in mud and drop it in to pluck the keepers off the top of the water. But we were legal. He had talked about some of his family being meat hunters up in the hills of Missouri—that meant if they were hungry, they shot and ate it.

He was really good on the bench because you didn't know what was gonna come out of his mouth. The players just shook their heads and laughed— "That's right Country, you tell 'em." And after regarding his words of wisdom in this book, I found out a hell of a lot more about what really went on down in the bullpen.

The stories in this book are not only humorous, but carry his voice which is purely southern Missouri, and will take you from his first at bat through his off-the-wall statistics. For me, this era was a big part of my life. The Royals was my first team to make it into the Playoffs as a manager. I was lucky, and so was Air, that we had this group of guys who filled in the cracks to make the Royals a winner. It was fun times.

When I was in Spring Training '66, Casey Stengel was the Manager. Billy Martin, Roger Maris, and

Mickey Mantle were teammates of mine. In one of the games, Casey, who was a real character, decided to hit me 3rd. Mickey wasn't feeling good that day, so Casey decided that Whitey was gonna be the three-hole hitter. I hadn't hit in the three-hole since Little League. The first time up, I grounded out. The second time up, I struck out. The third time up, I came up with the bases loaded and Casey, who was in the 3rd base box, called time. He walked toward me and I walked toward him and we met halfway between 3rd and home. I made eye contact and watched his lips move as he said, "Tra-la-la." Then he walked away as I turned and settled back into the box.

Well, I hit into a line drive double play, so after the game I caught up to Casey and said, "What did you mean when you said tra-la-la?"

"I was just tryn' to keep you loose, you know—tra-la-la."

I always tried to emulate and take Casey's style into my game as a Manager. He was a beauty. And in Air's case, he was loose in more ways than one. He wanted the ball and would generally bounce back the next day—he just wanted the ball. But for Air, he was definitely a different breed of cat that wanted to fit into any situation and be a part of this or any other team for that matter.

Through his off-the-wall statistics and passion for the game, it doesn't surprise me that he's still in the game and on the field. I'll say this, it's hard to make it to the show, but harder to stay. But this curious and whacked out kid from the country stayed with it and got some big league time between the lines while making the most of it.

As one last note, I wanted to make it clear that I did not give Mark the nickname "Airhead" because there was not "much up there," as he states. "Airhead" was just the coolest pitcher I've ever managed under pressure. He was a joy to manage, and a really good friend.

My Best,
Whitey

Whitey Herzog
Hall of Fame
Manager

Foreword Whitey's Take

INTRODUCTION

It rains hard in the Bootheel of Missouri, where I grew up. Florida has its Monsoon season, but in the bullpen at Cleveland Municipal Stadium, it poured. Cups of beer and soda were falling and sloshing into the grass, bags of popcorn opened up in midair as they floated down and were scattered like paratroopers coming in for the kill. And of course the half-eaten hotdogs were incoming grenades.

A true shower of shit was raining down on us. We all had made it back to the bunker where we were trapped, cut off from the field with no relief in sight. I'd never played Alamo before, and all we had for ammunition was baseballs, candy bars, and Copenhagen.

Now I'd gotten into a fair amount of trouble growing up, but this kind of reaction seemed to take it to the next level. Loud boos and angry shouts followed the trash into the pen. The whole right side of the stadium was up in arms and ready to come over the wall and we were still in the dark.

In the middle of this storm, a call came in on the bullpen phone. It was our manager, Whitey Herzog, who never, ever called down.

"Put Airhead on."

Introduction

BATTER UP!

I was born in the "Bootheel" of Missouri. These seven lower counties, hanging down into Arkansas and hugging the Mississippi River, produce over fifty percent of Missouri's entire crop. Soybeans, cotton, and water moccasins prevail; mosquitos are in the mix as well. I grew up in Gideon in the fifties, sixties, and seventies. Growing up there could be difficult at times, but we had our moments of adventure, escapades, and quite possibly some danger. Since this is the top of the Mississippi Delta, we have a tendency to bastardize the English language. We have a Southern twang that can trick a Mississippi boy, yet on occasion we will complete a sentence.

Gideon is where my passion for baseball took flight. It served as the background for my introduction to the wonderful sport at age six. Throughout my childhood, I could be found all over Gideon playing ball in sandlots, the backyard, parking lots, inside a barn, outside a barn, just about anywhere you could make up a field or throw, hit or rebound a ball off a wall.

I was six years old and starting the first grade when I got my first taste. Mom and Dad had been in the process of building a house right off good-ole No.5 Ditch, half a mile down the road from where my mom's folks lived which was in the Gideon school district. This was twelve miles from Tallapoosa (we pronounced it "Tal-a-poo-cee"), where my dad's mother—Mama Sally—was still living on the family farm.

It was 1959 we were living in Wardell, Dad was sharecropping and Mom was the school nurse in Gideon. I was a first grader and every school day I would ride the thirteen miles with Mom into Gideon. After school, I would take the school bus back to the Wardell line, and stay with a friend until Mom got through with her work. She would pick me up about two hours later, then we would truck back home where Dad and brother Eric were waiting to hear about the "big day at school." Eric was a year and sixteen days younger than me, and mischief quickly earned us the title of "The Gruesome Twosome." It was hot by the time it got to be summer, but you really never thought about the heat because we had fans everywhere—in the windows, on the floor, on the nightstands. Central air was, for the most part, cost prohibitive, we enjoyed going to both our grandmas' houses. They had those air conditioners that were stuck in the windows. Before the night fell, Grandpa Reiffer would have Eric and I help him round up the chickens to get in the coop. You got hot and sweaty, but there was nothin' better in the world than to stick your face in front of one of those air conditioner vents comin' outta the window.

That was the summer my Dad took me to play in my first baseball game. Well, really all I got out of it was an at-bat. Mom and Eric stayed home. It was probably the only game my mother would ever miss. Although my first at-bat was paramount, it was the "cat's Aunt Jane," as I would soon find out.

We started the trek from Wardell up to Gideon in the '51 Studebaker truck. As we were chuggin' along, still about two miles away, I saw these lights that just seemed to pop up and grow larger than life. We went through the bottom end of town, took a right, headed

over No.3 Ditch, went a quarter mile more, and—
Eureka!—we were now at the Gideon baseball field.
For the next twelve years, until I was eighteen years old
and went to play professional baseball, this was where
I would spend an incredible amount of time honing my
skills and loving every minute of this adventure, good
and bad.

There were cars and trucks all over the place,
but we finally parked the truck off the lane next to a
small ditch. (There are lots of ditches in the Bootheel.)
Walking up to the action taking place was way
impressive. The whole town must have been out to see
the show.

My Dad got down to business quick, and I didn't
have to be told to stay close. Most of the time, Dad
wore a brace on his right hand and forearm where
he had been shot up by a Czechoslovakian-made
burp-gun during the Korean War. He was a Marine,
so Eric and I had "yes sir" and "no sir" built into our
vocabulary early on. If you were standing on his right
side, you had to watch your step—he would swing
around on occasion and you'd be in the line of fire.
Getting hit with the metal brace was a big *OUCH*. He
always shook with his left hand—he was left-handed
anyway, as a matter of fact. He played catch with me
one time on the farm in Wardell. When he put the

glove over the brace it was tight and the impact of the thrown ball was, I'm sure, outta-sight pain. One year down the road, I would start throwing to Eric instead (and sometimes throwing at him). He would end up catching me anyway when we got older and played in high school, so I just started wearing his ass out at an early age.

Dad walked toward the dugout on the third base side and found the coach, Bo Wingo. Bo was the town sheriff, as he would be for many years. Bo was big—I remember thinking, "Nobody's gonna mess with this guy." He was still wearing that big straw sheriff's hat, just relaxing on the bench, taking a drag off his cigarette and giving directions to his team out in the field. I stood beside Dad as he stuck his head around the front corner of the dugout to get Bo's attention.

Dad hollered down to the other end where the big man was sitting, "Bo, you keepin' law and order on that bench?"

Bo stood up and said, "Hey, Alan, how you doing?"

"Just fine, Bo. I need to talk to you real quick."

"Come on down to the other end." We walked around to the other side of the dugout and Bo came out—man, he was big. "What's goin' on?"

"This is my son Mark—he's six and I know he's not signed up for Little League season," (it was toward the end of the season anyway) "but I would like to see if you could get him an at-bat."

Bo turned to me, "Hey, Mark, you wanna hit?"

I paused—my mind was saying, "This guy is huge"—but then the Marine, "Yes, sir," came out of my mouth.

Between innings, Bo went over to the other side to talk to the coach about getting me to hit with the other team. This was the closest I had ever been to a baseball field. I had never practiced with a team, or even swung a bat too much. Not against a thrown ball, anyway. The bat I had out on the farm was one of my dad's old bats and it was very big. Dad or Mom would underhand the ball to me in the front yard and I would swing, obviously trying to make contact. This bat stayed at home when we went to Gideon, but I did bring a glove. One thing that probably helped me get ready to hit a baseball was the fact that I always hit rocks and clods out of the driveway into the soybean field on the other side of the road. This was Mom's idea. One stipulation: Don't hit 'em into the front yard, too close to the house and all its windows. Melted sand and rocks were not a good mix. Same thing went for throwing. Eric was too little to catch the ball, so Mom said, "Go out in the driveway and throw rocks at the telephone line." The telephone line was across the road, so I had my work cut out for me.

Bo said to Dad, "Take Mark over to the other side, and they'll get him in to hit."

We walked around the stands—lots of people, lots of cars, lots of baseball. I went into the dugout where I didn't know anybody. It was kinda my first time being around that many kids my own age. It was like a big birthday party where everyone had a nice bat, a leather glove, and an opinion to boot. It was around the 4th inning that this tall, skinny guy came up to me outside the bench and said, "Mark."

I said, "Yes, sir."

"You're goina hit third, so be ready."

I didn't know what "be ready" meant, but I could count to three. Pitching for Bo's team was this kid named Pedro, and from listening to the other kids talk on the bench, this guy was pretty much unhittable. I had been standing up for half the inning before my first at-bat, trying to get a lay of the land and figure out what part I was supposed to play in this scenario.

Pedro got the first hitter out and someone said, "Mark! You're up on deck."

I didn't have a bat, but one of the kids said to use one that was leaning against the fence. I grabbed it and walked over to the white lime-lined circle. I looked into the stands at the crowd, and then turned my gaze out to the field at mighty Pedro. One of the kids yelled out, "You need a helmet on!" *Whoa*. I went back to the fence and picked one out. I'd never worn one of these, and thought it was kinda tight. All the way from the middle to the early sixties, equipment was for community or team usage. Every team had this one big bag that was packed with bats, helmets, catching gear, a first base mitt, and anything else that was needed to get the game underway. If one guy had lice we all got lice…nasty little critters.

This also would be my first experience with trash talk. A player from my side said, "Pedro's goina carve you up!"—whatever that meant. Eight years later, when I was fourteen or so, we would call this "talkin' shit."

Out number two. "Mark, you're up—go up there and hit."

I walked up gingerly and stopped about ten feet away from the batter's box. The umpire and catcher were a little intimidating with their masks, but the game must go on. I thought the umpire would say, "Batter up!" but all he said was, "Get in the box."

I got into the box, batting left-handed, and looked out at Pedro and waited. He wound up and threw the ball.

The umpire didn't have any trouble saying, "Strike one"—from what I know now, I was probably cutting into this guy's beer time. I turned to the umpire: "Would you care if I switched over to the other side to hit?"

"No problem."

I walked across to the other side, though I still had the left-handed hitter's grip when I moved over to the right-handed batter's box. I never thought about changing my grip. There were a few snickers coming out of the stands as Pedro wound up. Strike two.

Innocently, I looked up at the umpire again. "I liked the other side. Can I switch back?"

"No problem."

Now the stands and both benches were *howlin'*. I was back in the left-hander's box waiting for that last pitch. Pedro wound up and threw the ball—*but this time I swung and felt contact*. I had no idea where the ball went, but I made a right turn out of the batter's box and hauled butt at full speed down the first base line, hit the bag, and ran past it a little. I saw this on the Yankees and Detroit "Game of the Week" (in black-and-white, of course). Whitey Ford and Yogi Berra always put on a show. Al Kaline wasn't too bad either.

All of a sudden, everybody got quiet, and the first-base coach said, "Get back on the base—you got a hit. Make sure you run when the ball is hit."

I felt like saying, "I'm not a moron," except I didn't actually know that word at the time.

Standing there on first base, I had a big revelation. Nobody was hootin' and hollerin' at me now. *"Well holy cow, I kinda like this game,"* I thought to myself. *"So this puts people in their place."*

My time to shine ended quickly as Pedro got the next out, and I didn't get to go out into the field. The coaches came over to me between innings and congratulated me on the hit. They both agreed that I should come out to play next year, and I was nodding my head. Dad was waiting for me at the end of the dugout and said, "Good job. Nice hit." We hung around for another inning and then headed back to Wardell—but not without stopping at the corner Custard Stand to get a 5-cent ice cream cone. My destiny was now started; my brain was now in gear. What a great night.

THROW PEAS AT THE KNEES

NO PIES IN THE EYES

NO WALL BALLS

AND

YOU'LL BE JUST FINE

-Anonymous Redneck

BLOWIN' BUBBLES AND PLAYIN' BASEBALL

Getting my first hit on my first at-bat when I was six created this great aspiration. There was more to this craving; it was electric and it literally formed my overall demeanor and outlook on what I wanted to do for the rest of my life. That little pea brain of mine absorbed this game of baseball. It was an experience of mind, body, and spirit, and it would eventually come together and stay with me forever.

Baseball is a never-ending game of change. I never really thought about failure too much, but eventually the word "adversity" worked its way into my vocabulary. Without a doubt there is always something to learn from each player, each game, and each year. It's always going to be different…no two games are alike. The question is, "Will you stay young enough to see the changes as you grow older?" Nobody totally knows the game of baseball. This game is a democracy. It is formed by nine players with different roles, who have to make adjustments and deal with more adversity between the lines within each game. Good grief, this is the second time I've brought up the word adversity. What do I mean by adversity? Dealing with things you don't want or like to do.

Playing in the sixties and seventies would have been tough on anybody who had a trophy shop. Skeeter Kell Sporting Goods in Kennett had a corner on the "glitz and glitter" market. Usually somebody had to drive 25 miles to the south to pick up the wares. At my youngest age of playing organized baseball, we usually had 12 players to a team—that part is still the same today. In the playoffs, we had a winner and a loser for the town championship. We gave out one trophy to the winning team and then each team would have an MVP. Ten teams with an MVP award made it a grand total of eleven trophies of toy baseball players sprayed gold sitting on a wooden stand that stood eight inches high. Of course, the teams that won it all got a twelve-inch piece of glitter with a bigger wooden stand and a baseball that got sprayed up real pretty.

In the sixties, times were a little tougher for middle class America. Money was scarce so we fought hard to get to the top. Then, in the early nineties, baseball took a turn with its first hint of socialism. Some patsy-ass baseball board decided to give every kid a trophy... others followed and the world was lost. Well hell, I gotta raise my hand and call BS on this one. ("BS" is a common baseball term that stands for bullshit, but is not used quite as much as "are you shittin' me.") And we wonder why the millennial kids are so sensitive... should I pull out that word soft?

I can just see it: The somewhat educated high school or college student, diploma and degree in hand at that first interview realizing that it's the process that really counts. A few days pass as a call from the interview comes and they find out that they didn't get the position. Mom and Dad ask, "How'd it go?" with exuberance oozing.

"I think I finished second."

"But son, did you get a trophy for showing up?"

My take on this is that all this hardware does is clutter up the room. What did I do with my hardware? I gave it away—downsizing is great.

In small towns, everybody knows most everything about anything that moves, especially when it goes wrong. Gossip is thick. "Did you know Jamer Hilfiker got a ticket the other night when he floored it after coming out of South Side?" Or, "What about Freddie Fowler goin' fishin' down on the Floodway's Saturday night? Hell, he caught six catfish and a drum … man, what a day."

But any sport, especially baseball, was a big deal in Gideon. From the second grade through the sixth, it was time to play baseball under the lights twice a week for seven weeks. We played the fourteen-game Little League schedule in that hot, mosquito-infested area just east of town … one cotton field included. To quell these mosquitos they would start the foggin'. Yup, either the deputy or a city worker would bring out this foggin' machine that was combined with diesel and a dose of DDT, crank it up, then pull it behind the city's pick-up truck. Without a doubt, this would produce a nasty-ass smellin' vapor, a white fog that would rid the immediate area of those little bloodsuckers. It wouldn't last long, as they pretty much became immune to almost any concoction that was conjured up … they were just a damn nuisance.

On almost every Saturday night you could bet that the fogger was comin' out, because Saturday night under the lights was prime time for most folks to watch a ball game and catch up on the local chatter. A lot of young kids would have fun runnin' behind the fogger. That was until town sheriff Bo Wingo or deputy dog Jess Rudkin ran 'em off. You can bet there was no way they were going to have bed bugs and you could most definitely smell the ones that partook of the fun the night before in church the next morning. Oh, you're wearin' "Eau de Ballpark."

As I've said before, across the No.3 ditch just east of town was where I and many other kids would hone our skills to shoot for highest levels of play. It was kinda like playin' "King on the Mountain." Somebody would yell out, "Break up that double play," and if someone didn't like the way you slid into them, you might be duking it out before the last game of the night started.

Yep, baseball was taken very seriously in Gideon. My Aunt Bea would sometimes drive up and park down the left field line and watch the ball game. If someone hit a home run, she'd motion out the window of her Delta '88 and holler to one of the boys who was roaming around and not playing. She would call out, "Come over here, honey!"

"Yes mame, Ms. Bea."

"Honey, could you give this dollar to the player that just hit that home run? He did real good."

"Oh … yes, mame."

He'd go runnin' into the dugout yellin', "Ms. Bea just gave you a dollar for hittin' that homer."

If the hitter had time and was still in the dugout during the inning, he'd bust out of the dugout for thirty seconds and run down to where she had her car parked and holler either Ms. Bea, Ms. Polsgrove, or if he was really in the loop he could call her Aunt Bea, "Thank you for the dollar, gee thanks."

"Well, you did real good, sonny. You keep it up, you keep hittin' that ball."

If we were the winning team, the coach would sometimes buy us a snow cone for that winning effort. That was twelve dimes, and in my book, money well spent.

Bo Wingo was my first coach. He was as big as a house so he couldn't hit balls to you but he definitely kept us in line. Bo's dress for coaching was his khaki pants, khaki shirt, a Stetson hat, and sunglasses. He was your worst nightmare if you got pulled over in our town, especially if you were from out of state. If you got a speeding ticket, Bo would tell you to follow him over to the judge, who was a paraplegic. Bo would knock on the door, then go in with the accused and take a left into the judge's bedroom. This judge used to be a law student who had seen better days before a car wreck changed his life. He would weigh the scale carefully, fine you accordingly, then send you on your merry ass way, just like that.

George Scheider was my second coach. He was a Mississippi boy who taught history at Gideon High School. He was a devoted Baptist who laid the groundwork for all of us to improve our skill level, our attitude, and our work ethic both on and off the field. In other words, he would strive to build character. Coach Scheider would keep you in line on the field and lay down the law in school. He made a paddle out of rubber that I heard would make your ass vibrate. You only got on his bad side once.

George Scheider would wear us out until we got it right. He was relentless on doing it right until it became second nature. There was no running as punishment—if you screwed up, you just kept doing it over until you got it right. It's kinda like that in pro ball, too. He wore those big black horned-rim glasses (must have been a thing of the 60's). He had this burn-a-hole-in your-brain glare when he was frustrated with your performance, kinda like Superman. He set the tone and raised the bar for all of us to get better. Coach Scheider continued to teach and be the baseball coach in Gideon through my freshman year. Having a man of this magnitude around a small town environment was a real blessing.

FIRST PITCH OF SENIOR YEAR

The opening game of my senior year would be on our home field in Gideon, and we were playing Hayti. They had just won the state basketball championship. They were strictly a "run and gun" team. Most of that winning basketball team was now playing baseball and they had a few black players on the team that I had not seen before. Some schools in our area were 60/40 white to black. Very few were more black, but Hayti hovered around the 50/50 ratio. One thing to understand, in this area, the Bootheel, we all got along for the most part. We even socialized. Of course there were glitches, it was the sixties after all, but my brother and I didn't really care who we played—color or creed was never an issue.

It was the middle of March, and the temperature was around 50 degrees with a slight wind. It was a perfect day in Southeast Missouri for a home opener. This was a big day for me. This was my dream. To add to the equation, there happened to be three area scouts at this game—they stood out like a sore thumb. On our side we had every bit of 20 people in the stands, and on the other side they had a decent gathering of close to 12—just waiting for that first pitch to kick off the season.

The Gideon Bulldogs took the field and I took my eight warm-up pitches. Brother Eric, the catcher, threw down to second and "around the horn she goes" as Mike Nowlin, our third baseman, flipped me the ball. The first hitter was a black guy who was 6'3" and well built. He had this lean and mean-lookin' stature…a real stud. Eric was crouched down, the umpire settling in, but then I saw Eric lift up his mask and spit toward the hitter's shoes. I never knew why he did this, and he didn't do it all the time, just occasionally. He put the mask down and looked up at the hitter. I'm assuming Eric said something to him, because the hitter looked back and then forward toward me as the umpire motioned to "Play Ball."

Eric and I had an understanding with each other that had gone on for several years at this point of our playing days. We always tried to understand those certain little idiosyncrasies of the hitter, the umpire, or the opposing coach, to have that edge. Anyway, Eric motioned with the back of his glove and throwing hand to bring it on. There was no sign given, because hell yes, he knew the first pitch of the season was going to be a fastball, especially with three MLB area scouts wandering around.

I wound up and let 'er fly. It was a four-seam fastball that came out of my hand free and easy, so it was hot. This lead-off hitter stood in on the right side. The only problem with this was that the ball went wild to my arm side and came in like a laser to his head. The end result was a split helmet with the hitter laid out in front of the plate. He didn't fall backwards, he fell out forwards in front of the plate.

I thought, *"Whoa, he didn't even move when the pitch nailed him."* He went down like a bull elk. The lights were off on his side and I felt bad as I crouched down on the mound. The other team was now yelling that they wanted to kick my ass with all kinds of trash talk flyin' my way from their dugout.

Brother Eric decided to come out to pay me a visit while all the attention was directed toward the plate. The lead-off hitter was out like a light but rather than going around this very silent body, Eric decided to step over him as he made his way toward the mound. What I thought at times was now verified; my brother was a f'in barbarian.

I dropped my head and said in a low breath, "Are you shittin' me (a common baseball term)?"

Eric came up to me, took his mask off, looked down at his shin guard, then looked back up at me and said, "I told that SOB, 'You better hang loose, my brother can get a little WILD.'"

What a timely statement, Eric.

The player finally came around and they shuffled him back to the dugout. They eventually threw his ass into one of the parents' cars and took him directly to Hayti Memorial Hospital. Mom wasn't working at the hospital that day, she was watching her boys play baseball. But as always she found her way onto the field to be a caregiver. In due time, the game restarted, and it was "Play Ball" round two. The guys on their bench weren't chirpin' because I'm sure they didn't know if that pitch was on purpose or just a loose cannon ball. I threw a one-hit shutout. I had the whole plate.

LAST PITCH OF SENIOR YEAR

The Gideon Bulldogs made it to Sectional play and matched up against Sikeston, which would unfortunately be our final game of the season. Sikeston was 20 times the size of Gideon. We played in the VFW stadium at Sikeston, minus the cotton field. They were also the Bulldogs and had a very good arm in their pitcher, Don Miller, who had signed a letter of intent with the University of New Mexico. The game went the distance, but we had a mistaken pop up that landed in the infield grass for a hit. A stolen base and a misjudged fly ball hit with two outs was testy. Herman Huckabee was camped under it but it popped out of his glove and sent us back south. I felt bad for Herman, and he took it kinda hard. It was a 1-0 loss; close but no cigar. Sixteen MLB scouts were at the game. They would come and go, and they would keep moving to another game, just like I would.

Puttin' On A Show In Blytheville ... Gotta Get Drafted

After my last high school game as a senior, my brother and I were going to switch American Legion teams. We were checking out the Blytheville Cason's. First off, Blytheville, Arkansas was the same distance as Poplar Bluff, which wasn't really a game changer, although it was flat and straight delta ground. You could rev up the Big Block engine for sure. Blytheville was just off the I-55 and 40 miles outta Memphis. We would be more noticeable to scouts here than in the "Bluff."

They also had better BBQ. There was this place called The Dixie Pig and to this day they've been doin' their thing for around 90 years. They had the right idea on how to do up a hog.

Eric had two years left as a catcher, but I was planning on getting drafted so we were thinking more along the lines of their schedule. They had a few more games scheduled earlier than the Bluff and this would give me a chance to show what I had. There were always scouts runnin' around who might not have seen you … especially in this neck of the woods. This particular team had some top-notch players—they were a winning team with a 60-game schedule and had been in a State play-off tournament almost every year. Dwight "Red" Williams was the coach; he was also the head basketball coach at Blytheville high school. He had a following as an outstanding coach who knew how to run a game.

Both Poplar Bluff and Blytheville were about the same size, roughly 30,000, which was a metropolis to us. We went down to a practice and showed our wares—they warmed up to us and we warmed up to them. We liked these guys. Seemed there were a few more rednecks on this team, but we already knew quite a few anyway. The year before, when playin' for the Bluff, I threw 8 innings of no-run baseball against this very good Blytheville Cason team. We ended up losing, but Red Williams got a good look at me as a pitcher and Eric caught me that night. My hope was to pitch in as many games before the MLB draft, which would start on June 5th.

I got my first start with the Cason's on May 21st. We were playing Dexter, Missouri on our home turf at Light Brigade Field. Three of our top players would not be at this game, including Randy Smith (a left-hand pitcher who signed with the Angels the following year) and Glenn Johnson who were at their graduation. Then there was Tommy Fowler who was tied up with exams at Arkansas State. But that didn't matter to Eric and I or anybody else—play ball.

As most of us know, first impressions are what count. I gave up 1 hit and 1 run that was unearned. There's always room for improvement when you walk three hitters, but the 24 strikeouts got everybody's attention. I knew I had punched out a few, maybe 18 or so, but 24 was a heap. Eric missed a 3rd strike that ticked his glove and went to the screen, so to me it was a default strikeout. He and I had words in front of the mound—I told him to mix in a catch. "Hell, you knew what was comin'."

Eric said, "Screw you! Throw it and I'll catch it."

We won 5-1, and I end up throwing in three more games before the draft—pretty much lights out. I got drafted in the 12th round and signed on June 8th. But those Cason's went on to win the Arkansas State American Legion Championship, though they lost in the finals to Mississippi in Regionals. As the old Army song goes, "And those Cason's keep moving along."

MEETING
THE GANG

Being without a dog on the farm is tough. Growing up, we had Fritz, our longtime German Shepherd/friend who was present at many of The Gruesome Twosome's adventures. But eventually he passed away, and we were without a dog for almost a year. Dad came through and finally brought home a new German Shepherd pup. This guy had some big paws—yep, we knew right away he was gonna be a big one. To our knowledge he didn't bite. Yet.

Eric and I named him Count. My dad called him Damn-It. Yes, he had two names, but when there was food involved, he'd answer to both. This pup was extremely feisty and playful. He would always go for your legs, going through them and bumping up to the side. At right around a hundred pounds, he could put you on the ground fast. He would then hold you down and smother you for a few extra seconds of play. When Dad brought home our new pal, he was eight weeks old. Dad got the dog in Memphis, and—would you believe it—Count had a long, slow, Southern drawl on occasion. Only his would manifest itself in a kind of drawn-out howl. Maybe it was a genetic factor for folks of the South. Is it possible that the DNA had carried over to canines?

Damn-It/Count would end up being involved in my signing. In fact, it's safe to say that he set the tone for that momentous gathering. When the Kansas City Royals drafted me in June, Gary Blaylock was their area scout, and he would also be the one to negotiate and pull the contract together. Gary called up on a Tuesday and told me that I had been drafted in the 12th round. He then asked me if it was all right to come by on Thursday, around two o'clock, to talk about signing me to a professional contract.

"You bet," I said. "That would be fine." I didn't want to sound too anxious.

Sure enough, Gary arrived around two o'clock and walked up to the door. Damn-It came around the side of the house and eyed Gary. He was now almost eight months old, and a real go-getter. We heard a knock on the door, which quickly turned into a pounding.

"Somebody's in trouble," I thought.

Dad went to open the door, and there was Damn-It, tangled up under Gary's legs. (Dogs of this breed are known for protecting their masters. They can put a warm, yellow stream down your leg, real fast.)

But the topper was when Dad yelled, *"Damn-It, get out of here!"*

Gary's head jerked up and his eyes peered over the rim of his glasses, "What?"

Dad said, "No, not you—the dog. That's his name."

Gary got untangled and finally made it through the door. Yes, we got off to a real good start.

I ended up signing for $4,250. To add to the big day, I got four years of college with $2,000 a semester, which would be held in a college fund in New York by Major League Baseball. If I didn't use it, I would lose it. Additionally, Gary threw in an "incentive bonus." If I went to AA for ninety consecutive days, I'd get $1,000. AAA for ninety consecutive days, I'd get $1,500. If I made it to "the show" for ninety consecutive days, I'd get $5,000. Before we sat down, I'd been shooting for $6,000, but getting this college and incentive bonus, man, I was walkin' in high cotton.

Billings, Montana is a great place to be in the summer, and the Pioneer League was a great place to play a Rookie Ball season. There was hardly any humidity, and with night games in the mid-seventies, it was just about perfect. In 1971, there would be twenty-six players on the team, once all had filtered in, mainly from the West Coast. Joe Zdeb and I were the only two players from the Midwest. Joe was a fifth-round, high school pick out of the Windy City, and I had landed further down at number twelve. Competition was ripe, but we got along well. After all, outfielders and pitchers don't compete for the same playing time—I threw the ball, he caught it no threat.

When we came through that locker room door, all we really wanted was to size-up where we stood on the food chain. Six of the players were from the high school ranks, the rest were mainly made-up of college players from California. Jose Salas, a catcher from Venezuela, was the lone Latino. Bing Devine, a long time general manager of the St. Louis Cardinals for most of the sixties and seventies, said that scouting was like forecasting the weather—it's not an exact science.

I felt that I was a cultured, country kind of guy, but I don't think those West Coast college boys knew what to think of me, especially when I shook their hand a little longer than the normal dude, and declared, "Really glad to meet you," in my loud, Southeast Missouri twang. These boys out West probably weren't the kind to give you the old "steering wheel" salute. This was a simple greeting, when two trucks are coming at each other on the road—you know, the hand is on the steering wheel and the two fingers shoot up when eye contact was made, maybe even a nod—this acknowledgment is a style in itself, and will occur mostly south of the Mason-Dixon Line. My gut instinct was that these guys were borderline "Yankee." I didn't want to give 'em too much lead but eventually I was reined-in a little.

We were all there for the same reason, one we'd worked for ever since we could hold a bat or throw a ball—to play ball. And maybe try out some different food as well—food was an event for me. One thing I did notice was that about sixty percent of the team smoked. There were these sand boxes scattered between both rows of lockers—I didn't know so many athletes hit tobacco so hard.

Getting to know the players was…amusing. Sitting on a stool in front of your locker, you would hear a plethora (shitload) of topics being discussed. The first thing out of someone's pie-hole would usually be something like, "He's got good shit, but I'll tell you, that Johnny So-and-So…he's really got *really* good shit."

Basically everybody was talking about who had good stuff (their pitching arsenal: fastball, curve ball, change) and filling in the holes with a bunch of shit—common clubhouse camaraderie. When you'd walk into any clubhouse, your guard went up because you could sense the bravado elevate to a whole new level. I knew that I was in the right spot because the stretch of the most exaggerated story was always exceeded. Eventually, everyone started to talk and settle down…I think we all wanted to get a feel for and acknowledgment of, *Where are you from? Where were you drafted? Who the hell are you?* Etc. In 1971, we didn't have ESPN, Baseball America, or the MLB Channel. Sporting News was the "in" thing to read in the baseball world.

Because all of the players were coming in at different times, the first two days on the field were rather uneventful. Players staggered in at night, during the day, and even during workouts. Most flew in, some drove. All the troops that were there had an eleven o'clock workout at the park, and on that first day, we probably had ten players show up. The next day the number grew to sixteen or so. In baseball, by the way, you show up on time. The conventional wisdom is, "Show up ten minutes early and you're on time; show up five minutes early and you're late—zero excuses."

At seven-thirty, I ate breakfast at the Northern Hotel where we were put up for this mini-camp before the season started. It was June 12th, and we would open at home eight days later. I was in the locker room at nine o'clock because I wanted to get a good locker. We were also getting our uniforms issued by the trainer and a high school clubhouse guy who had no idea what he was about to get himself into. We'd end up going through two clubhouse guys in Billings in a two-and-a-half-month baseball season. With seventy-two games played and a whole lot of shit directed at the clubhouse guy (we'd call them "clubbies," among other things), they would have to develop a thick hide real fast.

The locker room was kinda small, around twenty-four by forty-five feet. I got the locker I wanted—it was about three lockers from the training room. It had a straight shot of most the lockers on one side, with a frontal view of whoever was coming into the clubhouse, and it was around the corner from the showers. Gary Blaylock's manager's room was maybe ten by ten feet and tucked away on the other side of the room. This was one of the places to stay out of—no shit. The shower room was around ten by twelve feet and had six showerheads that (amazingly) worked, but it didn't drain for crap. I was leery about the shower and kept my distance from the California dudes.

Our trainer was Mike Parker who was from Chicago and fresh out of college. That first day he was issuing uniforms with the sixteen-year-old clubby. We got pants and jerseys for both home and away games, a hat, blue stirrups, two pairs of sanitary socks (white socks worn under the stirrups), the pitchers got a jacket, and last but not least, a laundry bag. The pants and jersey were wool; old style, but the only style we knew. (I wouldn't see a poly uniform until Triple-A.) I got dressed—looked the part, felt the part—*play ball!*

I went out fifteen minutes early because my Dad was a Marine and he wouldn't put up with a slacker. The field, I felt, was great—it looked good, had lots of signage, and was better than anything I had ever played on in high school or American Legion. Of course, the first thing I checked out was the mound. I did this all the way through my career: mound first, dugout second. Once we stretched for three or four minutes and ran a few short sprints, we started throwing to knock off the cobwebs. We didn't go through a twenty-minute stretching regimen as we now do in the twenty-first century, but I was there to see it change, and change it did. Bullpens weren't done until the third day as we were split into two pitching groups. After throwing, our agenda for the rest of the day was to shag for what hitters were on the field, and then the pitchers would run.

Coming out of the flats of Missouri and playing baseball for the past four months, you would think that I'd be in shape. Well, with the higher altitude and running under Gary's lead. Once a pitcher in the show, and later the pitching coach when the Royals won in '85, Gary was determined to find out just how much mustard we had in those legs. I just hit a wall after fifteen sprints. Running as a pitcher in professional baseball gave a whole new meaning to "Let's get our running in." Thank goodness we finished at twenty. I was actually sore the next morning.

In the Minor Leagues, Gary was the manager and Mike the trainer (who would also act as administrator and held other numerous titles). Joe "Flash" Gordon was the hitting coordinator, Spider Jorgensen handled the infield, and Hal White and Bill Fischer watched over the pitchers. Gary Blaylock signed me, and was the also manager for the Billings Mustangs. The reason I got to go to the Pioneer League was because Gary had said when I signed that it would be alright to go up to Billings and play there rather than going to the Appalachian League, where I should have gone. The two reasons were demographics (I was closer to Kingsport, Tennessee), and there were more high school drafts in this league. Hell yes, I really was churnin' when he said Billings. I couldn't wait to explore the Wild West.

Gary was fair, consistent, and a borderline asshole. You didn't want to tangle with Gary. You definitely wanted him on your side. Gary was honest and extremely straightforward, and you really had to earn a compliment from him. They didn't want boys between the lines, so they needed somebody who could get the job done, yet still be able to develop... gotta keep getting better or you're gone. I remember throwing a no-hitter in high school and Gary and another scout were at the game. Gary knew what he was doing—he let the other scout talk to me before he would finish my ass off. He didn't say "good game" or "nice job"—what he wanted to know was why I threw a certain pitch to a hitter in the fourth inning on this count in this sequence. *Holy shit*, I just threw one of three no-hitters in my last year of high school, and that's what he wanted to talk about? I answered him calmly, but still went off half-cocked. I sure didn't think the Kansas City Royals would draft me anytime soon. Gary was extremely knowledgeable and would listen when you had a legitimate question, but he didn't go for guys wanting sympathy…maybe the trainer would listen, but hell no, not Blaylock. As we would say, he ran a tight ship.

In Walks George

Most of the team was in by the fourth day, and we had close to twenty-three players in an already-crowded locker room. The Royals' first-round pick was Roy Branch, a high school pitcher out of St. Louis, who signed and went to Kingsport, Tennessee to play in the Appalachian League. The second-round pick was a guy named George Brett, a shortstop out of El Segundo, California. Since his team was in a state playoff, George was going to be a late sign—plus, he held out a little. I was looking forward to getting to see what George was all about. His older brother John had played professionally and Ken Brett was in the Red Sox system. Ken was just getting ready to be a mainstay at the Major League level, and he would end up pitching for 16 major league teams. A lot of teams, a lot of trades. Bobby Brett was drafted two years later as an outfielder into the Royals system. I think everyone got the message that the Brett brothers were good baseball stock. I overheard that George Brett had signed and would be in Billings two days from now. A pitcher named Randy Johnson, also a high school draft from California (but not the Big Unit), knew George and somehow got wind of the arrival.

For two days we had team practice, going through BP (batting practice), infield/outfield, cut-offs and relays, PFP (pitchers fielding practice), and I threw in the pen. A bullpen was nice, because it meant I would be throwing to live hitters the day after tomorrow. Of course, afterwards we'd do our running and closeout with fifty pickups. A pickup is done with two guys: one guy has a ball, the other guy is out twenty feet in front. The guy with the ball tosses it fifteen feet to the left, and the other guy shuffles to get the ball, then picks it up with both hands, and flips it back to the guy that tossed the ball. The first guy receives ball, tosses it fifteen feet to the right, and the other guy shuffles over, then picks up the ball again, and this repeats forty-nine more times. In spring training, we would get up to a hundred for five days, then backed it down to seventy-five—monotonous.

Our workout had just ended and most of us were setting in our lockers, still trying to figure each other out. Suddenly, someone walked through the door, and Randy Johnson got up and walked over.

"Hey, George!"

"What's up, man?"

At least there was no "hey dude" at this point, but it would soon follow. You can bank on "dude" coming out of the West Coast. It was an old slang word for Eastern folk who were all decked-out and slicked-up.

George had a baseball bag in hand, stuffed to the hilt. His attire consisted of an almost worn-out El Segundo baseball cap, a t-shirt, shorts, and flip-flops. His dishwater-blonde hair stuck out from this salted, beat-up and shrunken cap. There wasn't a surfboard (unless he had propped it against the wall when he came through the door). Gary was in his office, watching everything. After he let a few of the guys extend their welcome, he raised his voice and said, "George, come on into the office."

George sat down and Gary gave him the ole "glad to have you aboard" welcome. Then Gary went through the rules of being a Kansas City Royal—in other words, he didn't like the flip-flops or t-shirt. Collared shirts and socks would be worn with all shoes—yes, George got the welcome and the message. It was hard to imagine that in fifteen years, George would become Major League Baseball's poster boy—at the moment, he only seemed to belong on the cover of a Beach Boys record. George and I finally met and shook hands, and I guess he was just as curious about me as I was about him. We probably both thought, *"What an interesting duck."* On the other hand, he probably had "dude" running through his brain…*"Is this dude a real, bona fide hick?"* No, George, I'm a cultured redneck. Let's get it right.

GEORGE IS GEORGE

I have to stop a minute here to say a few words about George. George Brett has been called a lot of names. If he were in an opposing ballpark and brought in the go-ahead run, the fans' creative name-calling side came out as expected. Should he be on home turf and doing damage to the opposing team, his name was repeated and yelled out in a much sweeter tone.

When Charlie Lau's name comes up in the baseball world, we think of one of the best hitting coaches to set foot on a field. Charlie was a hitting coach in the show from 1971 until 1984 when he died battling cancer at the early age of 50. Charlie had a lot of good Royal hitters in his corner, Hal McRae, Amos Otis, and Willie Wilson to name a few. I saw George work with Charlie; while both had a mutual admiration for each other, George (as well as a lot of Charlie's followers) had a deep-seated respect for a man of few words. When Charlie said something, you listened. Charlie gave George the nickname of "Mullet Head." A mullet is a vegetarian fish but George is not a vegetarian. A mullet does have a thick-lookin' head so Charlie, being the avid fisherman, told George, "I'm goina call you Mullet Head." He paused, and then came back with, "I might just call you Mullet for short."

George, as well as a lot of players, could be more than a little thick headed and stubborn at times. Many people who follow the baseball world know that George never hit over .300 in the minor leagues. A saying that I like which holds true for George is, "When the student is ready the teacher will appear." Keep your eyes open, listen, and keep searching for that teacher.

If you were to ask a seasoned big league player, "Who was the loosest player you've ever seen between the lines?" the response would be a slight pause, and then, "That's a no brainer—George Brett." George was a player's player, and many considered him the ultimate player. I was lucky enough to have signed in the same year and spent six years in the Royals system with him. We kinda warmed up to each other, probably because we were from opposite ends of origin—different folks, different strokes. He had sand in his pants; I had dirt in my ears. He was a beach boy; I was farm boy. Just two totally different scenes. There was one thing we did have in common. Even though we were a little crazy, kinda far out there, and goofy at times, both of us had this inherent passion to play baseball and even shine at times. Away from the field we were way off the norm by more than a bubble or two. We thought we excelled but we really didn't know any better.

Our Rookie season in Billings had ended. It was 1971 and we were going into our first Instructional League at our minor league spring training site on the outskirts of Sarasota. Most of us would pair up and get a kitchenette out on Siesta Key. Usually an older couple had acquired these small units and would live on the premises to make sure everybody's asses were kept in line. There would be two twin beds with a table that had plastic flowers stuck inside a vase of glued on seashells (probably made by the owner) as the décor. It was September and way hot. To hell with those glass vented windows that would crank open. We'd flip the switch and crank up that AC unit hangin' outta the other window. August and September had a sweltering heat, and when you added the humidity, it was slow roast with a baste. We were really excited about getting our Sundays off—we needed a day to rebound.

After the season, I ended up leasing a car and driving it down to Florida. I would be a commodity, or rather the car would. There were three times that George and I hung out on a day off and take in the scenery. The first outing was when we both agreed to drive east toward Myaka River State Park, which was pretty damn wild. Hogs, snakes, and alligators were the norm for this bordered-in jungle. We went east less than ten miles, and we saw very few cars. You could sense that this wasn't one of the highlights of Florida. But we were just exploring anyway. I went over a bridge with a good chunk of water extending in both directions. I slammed on the brakes, put 'er in reverse and got centered on the bridge to take a look-see at the scenery. George hopped out and was already lookin' at the layout. He punched me and said, "Look, there's an alligator on the bank."

I looked where he was pointing and sure enough it was just off the base of the bridge.

"Hey, watch this!"

I was thinkin', *"Oh shit, what's he goina do?"* He went down to the end of the bridge and down the side bank that had somewhat of a trail to the water. The alligator was camped on the bank, sunnin' himself. Well, somewhere along the way George found a stick and now wanted to play Marlin Perkins. (Steve Irwin the Crocodile Hunter wasn't around yet.)

"George…I wouldn't get too close to that thing," I called to him. It was at least an 8-foot alligator— definitely big enough to do damage. I could just see it now: *"Country—how'd George lose his foot?"*

Sure enough, George did his thing and the alligator held his ground. The gator looked to be in one of these séance modes, mouth open and jaw locked with teeth showing. George found this stick along the way and got close to his targeted prey. Yep, he whopped the gator and it hauled ass into the water. We had a good laugh and now I knew I could hang out with this dude. Oh boy, now they got me sayin' "dude."

Our second outing was when we decided to go fishing on the causeway that separated Siesta Key from the mainland. Right under the bridge there was this Marina that had a light over the water. We borrowed some gear from the folks that were renting us the apartments. We went one night around 8:00. It was only half a mile down the road, but I wanted to drive. I swung around to park as we wiggled through a spot that separated the fence at the water's edge. Hopefully this would turn out to be a prime fishin' hole. Light and water meant there's gotta be fish.

We were there an hour and ended up pulling in a five-pound sheepshead. We decided to go back, clean it and eat it. We loaded up and had this fish on a stringer. When George started to throw the fish into the trunk, I yelled out, "Hold it, I don't want that damn thing stinkin' up my trunk. You get in and I'll give it to you to hold out the window, it ain't goin in the car."

George held the fish outside the passenger's side window, and I scurried around the other side, cranked 'er up and we headed back. I didn't get 100 yards when I saw bubble gum lights in my rear view. I knew damn well I wasn't speedin' so I pulled over and got out of the car to face the fiddler.

George said, "Whatta want me to do?"

"Just hold your ground," I said, as I turned to face the policeman. "Hi, officer."

"What were you two doin' down in that Marina?"

I said, "Fishin'. Here, I'll show ya." I walked around to where George was and pointed.

George was still inside the car and said, "See, it's a big one!" He still had enough arm strength to lift it up to show off our trophy.

The officer laughed and then said, "You're not supposed to be in there. It's been broken into several times."

"Well, we didn't see anybody," I said.

This guy was startin' to laugh a little. "How about you guys go clean your fish and don't go in there to fish anymore."

"No problem, officer."

We made one last road trip. This time we decided to go to Busch Gardens in Tampa. First stop was the brewery, and then we went over and got some tickets to go see all these wild ass animals by train. But you can only see so many wild ass animals before it becomes boring. It was late in the day and the crowd just wasn't there so we made it up to where a few of the animals were caged. We were flittin' around here and there and walked up to this black panther that was in a hell of a good lookin' cage. This sucker was a big one and he was just lying there napping against the cage bars. I'm sure he had a big litter box.

Well heck, we were only five feet from this dude and the fence we were leanin' on was a little over four feet high. This cat was cool as a cucumber. Half his tail was outside the cage just swishin' back and forth, not a worry in the world. Until George said, "Watch this."

Before I could say "Tiger got your tail" George did a one-handed leap over the fence and yanked the shit out of its tail. This big black pussycat was now haulin' ass around the cage, while making some serious guttural noises. He was pissed off. George made it back over the fence pretty damn fast himself. We could see that you wouldn't want to do this in a jungle setting.

George was inducted into the Baseball Hall of Fame in 1999. The statistic that stands out for me and everyone else is that he is one of four players in MLB history to accumulate 3,000 hits, 300 home runs, and a career .300 batting average (the others being Hank Aaron, Willie Mays, and Stan Musial). Go George!

George – BATTLE READY!

George Is George

THE NEXT DAY AND DOWN THE ROAD

COUNTRY HAS ARRIVED

The day after George came in all the roving coaches and Gary were hovered around the cage watching these newfound pitchers and hitters show off their wares during batting practice. Roving coaches went from club to club within the organization and would come in spurts to make sure their specific players were going about their business and getting it done right. Spider Jorgenson, who was the infield rover, was off to the side hitting "fungos" to anybody on the dirt. Joe "Flash" Gordon was the roving hitting coordinator, and was glued into checking out the hitters. Gary would handle the pitching, and made sure things were in order to keep this field on the move and on schedule. All these guys had been around the game for ages. Woody Hahn, our young general manager, looked like he had rolled out of a frat house to check out the scene.

My mind was stuck on the throws coming across the diamond. Spider was on one side of the cage hitting ground balls to 3rd base, and Gary was on the other side hitting to a couple of guys trading off at shortstop. They were alternating throws to first base where Dave Landress was parked and taking the incoming throws. Dave was a UCLA boy but he was cool. There was a big square net parked out front of where he was taking the throws, to protect him from getting smoked by the hitter while he was occupied catching throws coming from across the diamond.

For two days, watching batting practice and shagging fly balls occupied my mind. Eventually I was told to take over the bucket to collect the balls, and then take 'em in and dump 'em into the throwing stand for the batting practice pitcher. He needed balls to throw and someone had to supply the ammo. I liked getting closer to the action anyway. There was also another big net parked behind second base just on the outfield grass so the man on the bucket would have some protection. The best thing about keeping the bucket was that I would be next in line to get loose in the bullpen to throw batting practice (BP).

My time to throw BP finally rolled around, and Craig Perkins, who would do the brunt of the catching during the season, would catch me. Craig played at USC (University of Special Children) and he was cool too.

After warming up, I went to the mound a little gun shy, but I knew I wanted to show my stuff. In other words, my thought here was, "Try to hit this asshole." About seven pitches into this batting practice, Blaylock came jogging to the mound and said, "Back it down, this is batting practice."

I didn't say this to him but I thought, *"Well hell, I've never thrown batting practice."* I've seen the coaches throw batting practice and then I was keepin' my eye on the others throwin' batting practice, and some of these guys were getting hit hard. So, I was thinkin', *"full throttle baby."* To add to the confusion I had to throw from behind this L-screen that had a net on it. Very confusing contraption.

Well, I backed it down and I was maybe 50/50 on balls to strikes. I kinda got the feelin' nobody wanted to get into the cage to hit my pitches. To top it off, the initial hitter trotted down to first and then took a lead off of the base. Gary yelled out, "Work out of the stretch." That was no problem I could see I had a runner on first.

Sure enough, the next hitter got into the cage and the dude on first was pretty damn far out there with his lead. *"Screw you, I'll just pick your ass off,"* I thought. Yep, I held the ball a little longer to bait him. Then I turned and threw over with an extra good pick-off move and put a little extra mustard on the ball with the ole "turn and burn" move—quick and deceptive.

Dave Landress was still taking incoming throws from across the diamond, but from my position he looked like he was holding the runner on first. So now he had an incoming throw coming from across the diamond and one coming from me on the mound. The poor guy had two white pills going directly at him.

The one throw from across the diamond was about a foot off the ground when it reached Dave, but he also picked up this white blur that zoomed by his head at about the same time. He froze into this half-ass squatting position. There was a pause in the action as everybody behind the cage was now laughin' their asses off. Our rovers Spider and Joe didn't let up for a minute or so.

Gary yelled out, "Hey, Mark! Just throw to the hitter, dammit." He jumped my ass before when I had called him coach two times in a row (he said to call him Gary or Skip, none of that coach shit), but the third time's a charm. So I hollered back, "No problem, Skip."

Dave came off the field at this point and was now in the dugout takin' a water break and shakin' his head. Then he disappeared and went into the clubhouse, probably to empty out his pants…he did go down into that half-squatting position.

Hell, I had never thrown batting practice in high school or American Legion. Woody, who was still the General Manager for the Mustangs, told me years later over lunch when I was back coaching in the Pioneer League that he knew I was going to play in the big leagues.

"How so, Woody?"

"When you tried to pick that runner off of first base during batting practice, my first thought was, 'This kid's gotta chance.'"

The next day Joe "Flash" Gordon kept asking, "Where's that Country Boy?" Well, I got somebody's attention and the name "Country" stuck as well.

When practice was over, we either walked back to our hotel where we were staying, or if you got to know a guy with a car and he let you ride, that was the way to go. We stayed at the Northern Hotel during this "gathering of players during this workout" stage. The Royals footed the bill for the stay during this mini spring training, but once the season started, it was up to us to find our own housing. Fortunately, we could stay at the Northern for $5.00 a night. Once we went on the road, any loose-end stuff could be put into a storage room downstairs.

During this short pre-season camp, we got $11 a day for meals, plus $500 a month for services rendered once the season started. In my case, services rendered would be throwing a baseball. The monthly salary started when the first pitch was thrown in the first regular season game and unfortunately would end on the final out of the last game. Not to mislead you or anything, but we got the $11 meal money on the road but not at home, and we had to pay $1.00 a day clubhouse dues, laundry and shoes polished. Make sure you tip the clubbie.

We opened up in Billings with a three-game home stand, and then we headed out on the road for nine days. You could see after the first home stand that we had some quality players and the makings of a good team. The tobacco chewin' was goin' full throttle on the field with the clubhouse sending up smoke signals as the butts were flipped into the sand boxes scattered around the floor. What was really cool was after each win at home we would each get two cans of off-breed beer. Since I didn't drink or chew at the time, I was virgin material. One of the college boys asked me if I drank. I said, "No, I don't drink."

"Can I have your two beers?" Everybody was lookin' for the win and the handout. Those college boys shot for all the angles to negotiate for a beer.

The next day during batting practice they'd start workin me. Rocky Craig, our center fielder, was the second to come up to schmooze me. "Hey, Country, if we win tonight can I have your beers?"

"Myron Pines already asked me, but maybe you can beat him to the draw tomorrow."

"Well, I'll ask you now for tomorrow."

"Well, let's wait till tomorrow, when I walk onto the field then you can ask me … I've gotta have some integrity too." That's when I became a low-key entrepreneur: I started trading two beers for a hot dog early on, and when I started drinking baseballs would eventually replace the beer. This barter system would follow me throughout my baseball career.

When we went out after a game on the road, most of the team headed to the one joint that either had pizza or burgers. The opposing clubby would give us the low down on places to go, and if it had beer, we gravitated there. Pool tables, shuffleboard, and foosball were throw-in's to keep us happy in that "Romper Room" mode. We liked to compete in anything. A lot of these guys didn't order a glass of beer, they just went ahead and got a pitcher and a straw. My niche was food, throwing down a few burgers was a warm-up, what really got my attention was a good stacked-to-the-hilt buffet. Yes, I was proclaimed to haul in the most food of any Mustang player.

I didn't get in to pitch until the sixth game of the year in Twin Falls, Idaho, but ended up with 87 innings, which would turn out to be the most of all the pitchers. With 5 wins and 1 loss and a 3.31 ERA, I had a productive year. Plus it was fun. When the season finished, we either flew out or drove out. Some of the guys we wouldn't see until spring training, then some would be lucky enough to go to the Fall Instructional

League to hone their skills further. Being asked to go to Instructional League was a feather in your cap. To keep up with any professional team you had to be young at heart and be on your toes, and this wasn't hard for me. I was nuts and nuts about the game. For a while, most everybody was on guard when around me. Especially Dave Landress. I tried to give him one of those "GO U-C-L-A" cheers, but that didn't go over very well.

The Next Day and Down the Road –Country Has Arrived

FIRST SPRING TRAINING

After the 1971 Rookie Ball season was over in Billings, I was invited to go to Instructional League. Being part of the Florida Instructional League would give you a little panache, you know, a feather in your cap. Back in the seventies, it started in the middle of September and ended around the second week of November. It was held at the Kansas City Royals spring training site in Sarasota, Florida. When I played, Instructional League went on for seven to eight weeks. Hum baby. After the regular season was over, this could be hard on the players, as well as the coaches, but we were troopers and would do anything to get a step up in the right direction. The adrenaline was still oozing. Florida was hot, humid, muggy, and when the pitchers weren't shagging fly balls during batting practice, the coaches would run our asses off for shits and giggles.

After "instructs," I took a two and a half month break before spring training started. Halfway through that break, I was ready to get going and see what spring training was really all about. In other words, I wanted to see if this dog could hunt in a big pack.

Two weeks before spring training would start, my ticket arrived and I was getting geared up to see all these new faces. Of course, my Mom started to pack the day after the ticket arrived. I didn't know what kind of message she was sending me, but I actually put my foot down and said, "Cool it, Mom. I don't need two big suitcases and half the barn going down to Sarasota." I know my Mom had my grandmother's DNA going full steam. It was hard to keep that Irish tribe held in check. My Dad was cool about it, he knew most of her antics but he also knew enough to stay clear. Eric was down at Mississippi State doin' his thing, so I was just in survival mode.

Two weeks passed, and it was like getting blood drawn every day. There's only so much pettin' the dog and huntin' you can do that could satisfy a life out on the farm. I was ready to go. I would work out for an hour or so, off and on, but I was goin' nuts and bored. Dad stayed busy keepin' me away from the mechanical gadgets that would chop off fingers.

Some of my girlfriends were scattered and went off to college. But one thing about these girls from the Bootheel, there was a pretty good covey of 'em that could walk through knee high corn and make it wilt. We were blessed. I made the drive north and south so they could educate me about their college experiences or maybe we could go out and watch the boat races a few times to see if the spark plugs worked.

February couldn't come soon enough. I was finally off to Sarasota. I flew out of Memphis with a stop in Atlanta, and on to Florida. I wanted to piss my pants I was so excited, but thankfully I held it in. When I arrived at the Sarasota airport there was a team bus that picked us up and took us to Hotel Sarasota. This would be the team hotel. It was a very old hotel that was eleven stories high, the tallest building in town, and stood next to Payne Park, the spring training and big league site for the Chicago White Sox.

They put me on the fourth floor and when I got there, I opened the door and laid my stuff on the bed to claim my space before my roommate arrived. I took the elevator down to the lobby, and got my first impression: though this was truly a grand old hotel, it had definitely seen better days. I would soon find out that the elevator either worked about half the time or was too full to be of any use. If you were waiting on an elevator that didn't work or running behind and had to rifle down the stairs, you were already in trouble. Who said we didn't have to apply "time management" into baseball? If you were late, missed the bus, or didn't get a ride with one of the guys who had a car, your ass was grass. Better get a cab and pay $25 bucks than to suffer the wrath of your manager. You'd get a fine, and have to run till you just about dropped. And worst of all, it took playing time away from you when you were only there to make a club to go north.

At night, you stayed close to the hotel. Guess you'd call this quality control. Especially with the 11:00pm curfew, and you had better be in your room during a possible room check. You did not want to get caught out after curfew. It was a very big no-no, anybody who broke curfew would start running when the team came together at 9:00 am. Those who violated this rule would run all morning till lunch, but first we would see their breakfast come up around 10:45. There would be a pause, a regroup, and then they would continue to run until lunch. Miraculously, I was never part of this group. I just didn't want to be coined a "shit disturber."

The Royals' minor league complex was fifteen miles from the hotel, toward Myakka River State Park just off of Highway 72. Back then it was pretty damn wild out there: rattlesnakes, wild pigs, alligators, red ants, and to make me feel right at home, they had a shitload of water moccasins on the grounds. When you drove up, the first things you saw were these two big ponds. Driving further you saw the office, players' lockers, cafeteria, equipment room, and training room all under one roof. The Royals' minor league complex was state of the art, definitely high cotton. It enabled the Royals to spread their roots to expand, yet keep many parts of the system close together. The Royals Baseball Academy, minor spring training, instructional league, the Royals rookie ball team for the Gulf Coast League, "rehab" for injured players, all took place on this site. There were five fields total. Four backed up to a tower, and the fifth field was the only one that was lit with very tall lights. The Royals had the best complex and fields, and other teams knew it when they came to play. The big league camp was two hours to the south of Ft. Meyers. Obviously, everyone's goal was to go south and be part of that forty-man roster.

Back in 1972, the pitchers and catchers would report to spring training in the middle of February at the minor league level. These days, they go the first week of March. Back then, we would get a full six weeks of spring training. Now they get three-plus weeks. Purely economics. Now they not only have Instructional League, but they pull guys in before the holidays for eight to ten days to see that they're following the off-season maintenance program. Then they'll do a pre-camp workout in January with a new group of players for eight to ten days, before they send 'em back home until March.

The first day out, we caught the bus at 6:00 am— don't be late. We pulled into the complex and the bus dropped us off on the cafeteria side. Whichever bus you got on was where the line started. The food was pretty damn good. Frieda, who ran the kitchen, ran a tight ship. She liked her boys eating well. But the chicks that worked the line could probably kick your ass. We heard they put saltpeter in the food so you wouldn't get to uppity or rowdy with the Florida female population off the field. Saltpeter, when put into food, basically says, NO PECKER POWER. It didn't work.

We didn't have much time to eat on that first day before we were shuffled toward the equipment room where Willis gave us our uniforms. Then we went directly to our lockers, and dumped our gear. I found my name on a locker and settled in. By the way, Willis was the equipment manager and head of the clubhouse. You did not want to piss off Willis.

The Royals didn't have our names on the uniform but they did give us a number. I felt glorified to be in this space. We read the board to see which field we would go to, got suited up, bullshitted for a while, told a few lies, and moved on. On the bulletin board was a notice that read: ALL PLAYERS TO THEIR ASSIGNED FIELDS AT 9:00 O'CLOCK. You definitely wanted to leave the clubhouse at 8:45. Just like before, if you were ten minutes early to the field, you were on time, but if you were five minutes early you were late.

I knew Willis from Instructional League. "Country, what number you want boy?"

"How's 14, Willis?"

"That's a good one," he said, as he took a drag off his cigarette and peeked over his black horn rimmed glasses. "Now scram!"

The first day on the field was more of a "Let's get your shit together" day. You got on the fields at 9:00, had lunch at 11:45, back on the field at 12:45, then off the field at 4:00. You'd put your dirty clothes in the laundry basket, get to the showers, throw your clothes on, then head to the buses. The buses left at the 4:30, 4:45, and 5:00, and yep, you did not want to miss a bus going back to the hotel.

At the end of the first day on the field, a few guys had turned white after running our sprints. We regrouped, caught our breath, and were all told to report dressed in our baseball pants, tee-shirt, sanitary socks, stirrups and tennis shoes, to the east of the cafeteria tomorrow morning at 7:00am. The whole camp would have a morning run before breakfast. This was repeated in Spanish for the Latinos.

Playing baseball is purely a ballistic movement, though in 1972 nobody used the term "ballistic movement" unless it was a rocket scientist. All they knew was, "Run MF'er".

The next morning there were approximately 125 players standing around next to the cafeteria in the dew-drenched grass waiting to see who was going to take us for a daybreak run. We all knew it was going to be hell for sure at the end of the second day.

A couple of coaches walked around the side of the clubhouse followed by this guy who was decked out in these shiny, flimsy track shorts and a white tank top that had KU on the front. The coaches called for everyone to gather around. We pulled forward to hear the morning words of wisdom.

"Gentlemen, this is Wes Santee. He's broken many track records in high school, college, and he was in the 1952 Olympics. He's from Kansas and we're going to turn it over to Wes now, so follow his instructions."

Well holy shit, the instructions were going to be simple.

"Follow me, because I'm going to run your asses right into the mud this morning. Yes, my name is Wes Santee and I'm going to take you on your morning run."

There were no lines of three or five running in an orderly fashion. This was a "Braveheart" charge. In this mixed group of stallions we had some runners, a few trotters, some walkers, and yes a few nags that broke down along the trail. In baseball, if you want to rattle someone's cage, do sprints. Short bursts of stop and go with little time to catch any air in between can drive the point home pretty damn quickly. Yep, I'm sure our clubhouse man Willis was not pleased with all the mud carried in on the uniforms. He was probably suckin' down an extra pack of cigs and cussin' under his breath: *"What the hell, just look at what this skinny ass track star has done to these uniforms! Just look at this shit!"*

Conditioning really sucked, especially because none of us felt like eating after running through that morning mud, it left our guts in a knot all day. We were all extremely happy when Wes Santee moved on after just three days.

The 300-yard shuttle was another running exercise that really got us going. This workout would get your blood pumpin' pretty damn quick, almost deadly. You'd set a cone out 50 yards from the starting line, with a coach on the line, and one on each cone to make sure the runner touches both the cone and the line. Generally, there would be eight stations (cones) set up, as "Pure Hell" was getting ready to start. This little trial would set a standard on how much work you had put into the off-season. The test was based on weight, with a time matched up to how much you weigh. Let's say you're 210 lbs., then you had to perform the task, at say, 54 seconds. If you don't make it, you go to the fat farm. That means coming in on the early bus at 5:15, working out with the strength and conditioning coaches, and then three or four days later you'd be going at it again, until you make the grade. Believe me, you definitely wanted to make this on your first try.

We were all situated with the team that we would play with once spring training broke. There wasn't much player movement until maybe a week before each team broke to go north (which meant anything above Sarasota). There were four minor league teams; two A ball teams: one in Waterloo Iowa, the other in San Jose, California. The double AA team was in Jacksonville, Florida, and the triple AAA team was in Omaha, Nebraska. I had just turned nineteen in January and I had a strong feeling that I was going to settle in at Waterloo.

In Florida, I realized right away I needed to start separating myself from the good, bad, and the ugly. I knew I had to hang with the right crowd, make it to the field on time, and make sure not to forget my jacket, cup, glove, and especially my brains.

Everyone was on a specific field on time, no excuses. "Coach, I was in the training room." Tough shit. "I was in the bathroom." Tough shit. "I had to run back into the clubhouse, I forgot my jacket." Tough shit. The "Tough Shit" category was not one you wanted to fall under because now you were a turd and there's one thing about turds: YOU CAN'T POLISH A TURD. Also in pro ball, you did not use the word "coach." We called them by their first name, or called 'em "skip." No Mommy's and Daddy's around this field.

There were 31 players on the field for the Waterloo team. But whoa, they were only taking 25 players north! Being an ADD guy (though I didn't know it then), I wasn't particularly good at math, but I did figure out what was going to happen to the other six players. This was real competition, no BS, and you definitely didn't want to get on anybody's shit list.

With 15 pitchers and 16 players on field #3, when camp broke on April 2nd there would be 11 pitchers and 14 position players that went north, with three of the position players being catchers. In Rookie ball, you have a 72-game schedule, but at the full season level you play 140 games. We called August the "dog days"; believe me, in your first full season you will suck air, especially when it gets hot and humid.

Steve Boros was our manager, and I got to know him in the fall instructional league. Steve was a perfect fit for me; he was well educated, had played with the Detroit Tigers, and a class act. He just wanted to get you better.

We all made it to the field on time. Steve walked up and started chewing the fat with us and at 9:00am he said, "Let's go, gentlemen, everybody over here."

As we huddled up, he greeted us and let us know that Waterloo, Iowa was in the Mid-West League. That meant it was cold early and hot and muggy from the end of June on. And it rained. His lay out was simple: "My job is to get you ready to go north and get you better to move on to the next level." He didn't threaten anybody or let us know that, well, we had too many players on the field and some of us wouldn't be here in six weeks or sooner. Instead, we just got down to business.

Usually we would have a coordinator drop by and help out or observe what was going on with the teams. They would rotate through and maybe throw some batting practice before breaking for lunch. A coordinator, or "Rover," was broken down by position. You would have one in pitching, one in hitting, and one in fielding. The manager at this time would control the catchers and outfield play, but as the game progressed over the years and as it grew, so did the number of instructors, and the quality of instruction. It was close quarters with four fields backed up to each other, so there wasn't a lot of running from field to field for the Rovers. Back in this era of baseball, it was the manager, trainer, and the bus driver (bussy) when we went on the road. We knew exactly what to do and with one head honcho on the field, you did as he told you. He'd treat you like a man unless you chose to act differently.

The trainer stayed in the training room or in the dugout until somebody went down. We didn't have strength and conditioning guys. We didn't lift weights, we just ran our asses off...killer shit. The trainer didn't lead the morning stretches, or any other stretch for that matter. Steve led the first two or three days and set the tone, then two or three college boys that were literate would repeat the format. Toward the end of camp, I would come forward to lead. I got a change of scenery and felt like I had spread my wings some. I established myself and I would break camp as the opening day starter.

The Royals were probably one of the first teams that were innovative in so many ways and tried to set themselves apart from the generic approach to professional baseball. They have been called the team of the seventies.

After we stretched, Steve said, "Huddle up. We're going to throw and pitchers, once you start stretching it out to a hundred and twenty feet, let's start throwing the ball on the line. We don't want any humps on the ball. We'll throw about ten minutes and then shut it down. Do not try to impress me during the throwing program. Impress me between the lines (game) when it counts. Both sides will start at the same time—do not start until I tell you to start. Pitchers on the right field line, position players on the left."

We paired up and threw for ten minutes. Then we went through at least 45 minutes of cut offs and relays. This was one area that you can keep going over and over and it never seems like it's done the same way twice. Forty-five minutes before lunch was batting practice and of course, the pitchers were spread out and shagging balls. We usually played our own games of catching fly balls to keep the boredom at bay. The first one who caught three fly balls won. Or, when you were really with it, you caught the fly ball behind your back. It hurt like hell when you got hit on the wrist instead of the glove. You got the hang of this quick or didn't play. Coaches have eyes in the back of their head, they really don't miss anything.

For six more weeks, we showed our stuff, but the true test came when the spring training games started. There were a few tight assholes, but it was play ball and show off your wares. Five days after our first bullpen, we were playing real live baseball games.

Forming any team is about figuring out which 25 guys can play and work well together. The luxury of having the ultimate 25 players is definitely not always the case. Granted, the Royals knew where you were going for the season, but it was the manager's job to keep the chemistry in balance.

A lot of guys wrote their own ticket home, or at least out of camp. They just didn't do the little things. Paying attention to detail was a big objective...but then you had to execute. At this point, it's those little things that separated the player from the wanna-be player. Retention, recall, ability to adapt, intestinal fortitude, the danger of peaking, just a lot of bumps in the road. We weren't going between the lines to finish second; nobody wants to stand up and start yellin', "We're number 2! We're number 2!"

No, what we wanted to do was kick ass and take names, eventually have a beer, talk some baseball, or check out the local female population, and then call it a day.

Bill "Fish" Fischer was one of the most interesting characters anybody would ever encounter. He was a scout with the Royals, and followed the pitchers in spring training and during the season. He played the game professionally for nine seasons with five different teams. He holds a record for pitching 84, 1/3 innings without walking a hitter. He was a scout, pitching coordinator, big league pitching coach, and now he's an advisor. When you first met Fish, you'd think that he should be on an Army poster as a drill sergeant. To me, Bill Fischer was the closest thing to Yogi. Yogi had Yogisms and Fish had Fishisms.

I remember meeting him at my first Instructional League. He had all the pitchers doing the six-inch leg lift and hold. I thought it lasted forever. I had (and still have) a very good core but I guess he wanted to see our breaking point. The whole time he was yellin' "Keep 'em up." This was done at the end of the day, and we knew he was trying to kill us. Then all of a sudden he started to walk and step on our stomachs before moving to the next guy. He acted like it was no big deal, walking around with a shit-eatin' grin.

Fish moved on to be a big league pitching coach with Cincinnati, Boston, and Tampa Bay. He picked up some time to help out John Schuerholz in Atlanta to get their young pitchers on a roll. Roger Clemens was in Bill's corner as his pitching coach during his tenure with Boston. As a scout and advanced pitching coach, Fish would make his stops in the AA and AAA towns to check on his pitchers (and pitching coaches), usually staying for 5 to 6 days.

There was one thing nobody liked when Fish came into town. After the game when we usually had a spread out on the table. Fish was generally the first one to the spread. We didn't mind this part, but when he walked up to the spread in his birthday suit, with the towel crunched in his left hand and riding on his hip, it was a real scary sight. Yeah, see the towel thing, well, it just wouldn't go around the watermelon that protruded forward from his back. We just dropped our heads when Fish moved through the line to get to the salami, mac and cheese, anything that looked palatable. I'm tellin' ya, he was right on top of the table, very close proximity to the chow. It looked like he was draggin' body parts through the spread; no knife needed to spread the mustard or mayonnaise. Some would take their chances, but then most of us would go out for burgers and a beer instead.

After more than six weeks of competing for a position, the final roster was set three days before we broke camp. It was all about development, so the Royals took the best 25 players north that were a fit for the Mid-West League. Our team was in Waterloo, Iowa—Yee Haw, lots of corn. We got a 140-game schedule to play, maybe a few play-off games if we made the grade. I came in alone on a plane and flew out with the team when we broke to go north. It got extra cold in April, especially since most all were night games. When it got hot, one thing that made me feel at home was when we were playing in Clinton, Iowa. It was on the Mississippi river. Right at game time, when the sun had just set, the truck pullin' the mosquito fogger start movin' slowly around the park. I spoke up and educated the California dudes. Yep, those bloodsuckers were out and about, and you could find 'em everywhere.

First Spring Training

SEPARATING YOURSELF FROM THE PACK

The Mid-West League was a bittersweet experience. Thank God that A Ball in Waterloo, Iowa was over. I was our opening day starter and would throw a 3-hit shutout right out of the chute and from there on it was a roller coaster of ups and downs for the remaining 139 games. Yeah, I made the All-Star team and led the league in strikeouts, but with a 10-9 record and 3.47 ERA, I wasn't exactly setting the world on fire. There was just no consistency. Maybe there were too many corn people.

Now it was September 1972, and I was back in muggy Sarasota. This Instructional League was my second go-around, and close to half way through the league I started feeling like a mule had kicked me in the head and knocked some sense into me. I started to grasp a technique that would rein me in and move me forward and up the ladder rather quickly.

One day, the whole team sat in the cafeteria waiting for a mandatory meeting. Hell, they were all mandatory. We waited for five minutes or so, and in walked Dr. Bill Harrison, who was an eye doctor. Bill would be one of the first, if not *the* first, to develop and enhance how an athlete can control the brain and the senses, with emphasis on the visual aspect. Basically, if you could slow your grey matter down, you could quite possibly have a great run between the lines.

Dr. Harrison was followed by two other doctors who would also play a role in getting us to make our bodies and minds work and flow in the right direction. There were close to 40 players in this room, and we were all a little curious about what was going down. These three guys were "Ivy League," making this a kind of water and oil scene. You could tell they tried to dress down but that didn't work. They all wore creased, lightweight woolen slacks. Two had laced leather shoes that still had a shine, one had a monogram on his sleeve and to top it off, one held a pipe in his hand. Two of them pushed their hands through their hair on several occasions—I thought this might be an attempt to push their brains back into the cranium. Yeah baby, we were goina go full throttle with the academic Larry, Curly, and Mo.

They were there to give us their spiel on how they could maybe make a difference and help us enhance our game between the lines. Bill stepped forward and introduced himself and the other two gentlemen, then cut to the chase: "How many of you guys would like to learn to 'concentrate' better between the lines?"

A little over half raised their hands, and he continued to explain and lay out his plan to hopefully push our performance to the next level. Eventually, the other two doctors chimed in, but Bill was calling the shots and trying to give us an idea as to why we might want to look into this newfound technique. "Hear us out, and see if it could help you, or at least fit into making your game kick up a notch."

He gave us a few examples how we would normally look at an at bat or what the pitcher might be focusing on when delivering a pitch. What do the eyes relay to the brain between the lines—better yet, under duress? Was there a plan between the lines? The common mindset would be, "This is what I've got today attitude and I'm doing just fine approach."

Was there a plan or a goal to follow? Getting your bat blessed, jumping over the line when heading to the mound, or eating six Twinkies and a hot dog went out the door as part of your game plan.

Bill emphasized that pitch command was a byproduct of focus command. He asked us, "How many of you have a physical plan for pitching?" Nearly everyone's hands shot up. He then asked us, "How many of you have a focus plan?" No one raised a hand.

"So, if you can believe that a loss of focus precedes the release of the pitch when you don't have pitch command, perhaps learning about and developing a focusing plan could be of great value to you."

Well, not all of the players were willing to try this new methodology. About half of us jumped at the chance to test the waters and see how we might get over a hump or any obstacle that stood in our way. We did several eye exercises, drills, a few exercises using a trampoline, and developed our own tailored routine. The goal was to eventually bring us into focusing at an optimum level when going full throttle from the first pitch until the last out. I needed an edge; I wanted to learn to calm my mind between the lines, under adverse conditions, where it really counted.

Bill said, "If you're a starting pitcher, you may throw 100-120 pitches in a game. Your focusing plan needs to be consistent and something you apply on each pitch, no matter what the circumstances may be."

He went on, "What do you do when you are pitching well, when you have good pitch command?" Without giving us time to answer, he said, "I think you likely use, without knowing, a four step plan. You analyze the situation, you visualize the pitch you are going to release, you center your attention on the target, and you execute by maintaining focus on the target and letting it happen."

After about two weeks of my undivided attention to detail, I started to see, feel, and grasp this method. The very first time I applied it was against the Pirates Instructional League team. In three innings of work, I walked one but struck out nine. I was calmly focused and felt no pressure. The time I had spent between the lines that day was noticeable. I wanted to improve, and worked at my game off the field, pushing my mental capacity to help deal with duress under fire. I didn't have to go between the lines to work on this. I relaxed my body and took my game to the mental side, imagining how I would react to a tough situation, or take it even further to a worse case scenario that I had created. This was all done in a very quiet place, with my eyes shut, and my mind creating a clear, vivid picture of any situation I would choose. Dr. Harrison calmly woke me up, and many more would follow.

On the second day of the '73 spring training camp, Lou Gorman and John Schuerholz (the assistant farm director) who were attached at the hip, walked down the runway toward the center tower when I jogged in to change my shirt. As I caught up to them, Lou stopped me and said, "Mark, you're always in shape."

I said, "Yes sir."

"Arm wise, are you ready to go between the lines?"

"Yes sir."

"Well then, could you go over and throw maybe 3 innings tomorrow with the AAA team?"

I said, "You bet!"

"The big league team hasn't sent any pitchers down and we're short, so this will give you a chance to see what a higher level looks like...maybe give you a feel for elevating your game," he said. "Go ahead and report to field 5 after lunch. Harry Malmberg (who was the manager at the time) will be expecting you."

"Thanks Lou," I said. "I won't let you down."

By the way, John Schuerholz would become the GM for the Atlanta Braves a few years later and they would rule baseball for a decade—it was a dynasty. To top it off, John had a '69, 442 Oldsmobile convertible that I knew would absolutely haul ass. Anybody that liked to haul ass in my book was cool. Both he and I were deaf in one ear so we repeated ourselves a lot with elevated voices.

I pitched the next day and ended up throwing 4 innings, 2 hits, 2 walks, 0 runs.

After the game, Harry said, "Nice job, young man."

Little did I know that Harry had asked Lou if I could stay with him for another outing, so I remained with the Omaha AAA team until I pitched again, three days later. I threw another four innings with about similar results. Harry said to Lou, "Why don't you let Mark stay with me until we break camp?"

Lou was emphatic with Harry that Mark Littell would more than likely be going to Jacksonville AA and be the opening day pitcher. Harry tried to change his mind, but Lou said, "Harry, he's going to AA Jacksonville. No ifs, ands, or buts about it. He's thrown 8 innings for you but he'll drop off. We've got five more pitchers coming down from the big league camp, you'll see."

The last game I threw in spring training was a 9-inning, 3-hit shutout. Lou was at the game and in the eighth inning I saw him shaking his head. After the game, he pulled me off to the side and said, "Young man, you've had one hell of a spring. Believe me, you have been the talk of spring training. Now against my judgment, I'm going to go ahead and let you break camp with Omaha."

I was outwardly calm, but inside I was beyond excited. I wanted to burst. "But Mark," Lou warned before I went off. "Should you get off to a slow start, we'll get you back to AA Jacksonville."

Bill came in and saw the team and me in May. I was 4-0 at the time. To be in this mix was a mystery. It was 1973 and early in the season and I didn't go to big league camp, so I was not a 40-man roster guy, much less an invite. My first game was in Denver, and it was the biggest launch pad in all of baseball. With light air and miles of space, Mile High Stadium was not friendly to pitchers. I threw 7 innings and gave up a lone solo shot in the 4th inning to Cliff Johnson that was golfed 6 inches off the ground.

Tommy Harmon, who was catching me, came out and said, "I gotta shake your hand, that is without a doubt the longest fucking ball I've ever seen hit." Cliff's foot was touching second base as the ball had peaked. Yeah, he got it.

This jump from A to AAA happened in a short span of time—only seven months. I began performing better than I ever had, and I believe that the moment it clicked for me was learning Bill's methods. Bill Harrison jolted what brain I had and made my time between the lines enjoyable. I used to sweat too much and work too hard. After learning then applying this new approach, my mantra might be stated as "work easy, work smart, and slow down. Know what you can do and also what you cannot do." Then execute. This mental approach served me well in the years to come, and helped me separate myself from the pack and move into the big leagues. Who said this dog can't hunt?

By June 9th I was 9-1, and I got the call to go up to the parent team. George Brett and Buck Martinez, who I roomed with, were glad for me. Both George and I were 20 years young and having a blast. He was especially happy for me, since we both took a lot of guff from some of the older players.

BLUE ANGEL

Indianapolis, 1973

After my big first AAA win in Denver, I kept on feeling my way through the league, just packin' on the innings and taking no prisoners. It was "Oh-eee-Oh" off to work we go, and lovin' every minute of it. One month later, when I was 5-0 and living the life, we were playing in Indianapolis. The Indianapolis Indians team was the AAA affiliate for the Cincinnati Reds. Owen J. Bush Stadium was a nostalgic old ballpark that had some flair. It had a brick wall and looked like "The Natural" might have been filmed there—it fit the part. The team was a good one; a lot of these guys would be part of next year's "Big Red Machine." Joel Youngblood, Dan Driessen, George Foster, Ed Armbrister, Rawly Eastwick, Ray Knight, Will McEnaney, and Joaquin Andujar—pretty damn good bunch of players. Their manager, Vern Rapp, would even be my first manager when I was traded to the Cardinals.

Dennis Paepke, "Pap," was catching me that night, and he was the one with the most tenure. He was also the meanest—don't cross Dennis, you want him on your side. It was the first week of May and the weather was warmer. I thought to myself, *"I can dig this, one step out of the show; I'm 5-0 and catching a lot less shit from the older players."* I felt pretty damn good.

I was coasting along but the umpire was making it a little tough on me. Still, I wasn't going to start showing up a AAA blue much less any umpire…you want those guys on your side, too. If we didn't know the umpire on a personal basis, we called them blue, since 99.9% of the time their uniform color is BLUE. In AAA, you have three umpires; AA and below you have two on the field, a plate and field umpire. In this particular game, the umpire wasn't giving me much of the plate, and I could tell Dennis was starting to get a little irritated.

Pap was talking to the umpire behind the plate and I couldn't help but notice that he'd put a mark in the ground with his index finger—this was happening about every other hitter. My body language was generally pretty good but I felt I was getting squeezed.

I threw in a few disgruntled facial expressions to chime in on the disappointment of his strike zone. I thought, *"This boy blue needs his eyes checked!"* I was about ready to go up and tell him to punch a hole in his mask to see the incoming.

A couple of pitches later, Dennis put another mark in dirt but this time he stood up and turned around. As he swung around to give the umpire his two cents, you could see his mask come off. The mitt was in his left hand, the mask in his right, Dennis's back was to me but I could tell they were going at it for about 15 seconds. What I would find out after the game was that Dennis was putting the marks down in the dirt as a way of saying to the umpire, "Yeah, you missed another one."

Dennis went back into his crouch and put a third mark down into the dirt when all of the sudden, this blue boy of an umpire with his arms crossed, bent over and said, "Hey Paepke, you get to five and your ass is grass. You're gone."

Paepke turned and said, "Oh yeah? So now you can count."

The umpire glared but Pap didn't say the magic word, so he was still in the game. I got the next hitter out for out number two. Dennis called time and came to give me a little comfort … yeah, right. Instead, he said, "Country you're throwin' just one hell of a game. You feelin' pretty good huh?"

"Yeah, sure," I said.

"Here's what I want you to do. Give me your best fastball right down the middle. Throw it right at my mask."

Well, that was no problem for me but the number five hitter was coming to the plate and every once in a while he'd run into one. That hitter was Roe Skidmore, and he too had had some time between the lines.

I said, "Pap, Skid's goina smoke it."

"Listen," Dennis said. "I'll take care of Skid. You just throw right at my mask. He never swings at the first pitch anyway." As he started to walk away, he turned for a second and said, "Don't forget… let'er fly."

Skid was just outside the batter's box stretching with his hands above his head as the bat dangled behind him. Pap bumped into Skid before he got into the batter's box. He took his place behind the plate, kinda lookin' over the situation as most catchers do. But there was no situation. Nobody was on base, and behind that mask he probably had a big, shit-eatin' grin. I would later find out that when he had bumped into Skid on purpose he said, "Skid, how about lettin' the first one go?"

Skid's response: "No problem."

Dennis crouched down and set up. He didn't even give me a sign; all he did was motion with his glove and right hand—both hands moving like he's lining up a freightliner truck to back up. Basically he was saying "Let's go, let 'er fly."

I wound up and let 'er rip, just like Pap had said. Roe Skidmore didn't swing at the first pitch, and the ball went between Dennis's mask and mitt. But as I was watching, something funny happened. The baseball gods came into play on this one really quick, and all of the sudden, this umpire fell backwards onto the ground and landed spread eagle. The ball had hammered the lower part of his mask and pushed against his jaw, kinda like taking a one-two punch from Ali. This guy was out, stone cold.

I walked up to the plate area and Pap said, "He looks like a snow angel."

I responded, "No, he's a Blue Angel."

I had thrown what one would call a heavy fastball; the pitch had real good rotation with plenty of RPM's on the ball. Catchers always let me know that I was not fun to catch. To add to my flavor, I was also what you might call, "conveniently wild" to top it off.

Both trainers came joggin' out to see why this guy was looking straight up at the stars, not moving, with his mask still in place. The other two umpires hovered over their buddy, plus there was a small covey of folks starting to form around the plate. Even the team doctor came down out of the stands. For about a minute we were on the field and then realized we should go to the dugout and take a load off. We could see that this mishap was going to take a while.

We went into the dugout, and though nothing was said, the thought had circulated among the other players. Harry said nothing to any of us about this trip off the field, but we knew what everyone was thinking. A minute later, Pap was smilin' and suckin' down some water, saying, "Yeah guys, Country and I got crossed up." Right.

Another few minutes later, the umpire in question stood up, groggy and lethargic. There wasn't an ambulance yet, but the other two umpires and the trainer for the home team took charge. What a sight to see. I was sittin' on the bench watching these two umpires holding this guy up just weaving their way along the 3rd base line then continuing to head up the left field line toward the umpire's room. My take was three blind mice having a tough night but the one in the middle just got the shit kicked outta him. Dad and my high school buddy Jamer Hilfiker were at this game and they were both just laughin' their asses off. Dad said it was like watching three drunks after an all-nighter.

After about five minutes or so, the umpires came back out one man down, and the game resumed in the fourth inning. We headed back out to the field where I threw a few needed warm-up pitches, and the game got back underway. It was probably close to 15 minutes before the new umpire motioned to play ball.

Roe came back up to the plate, but before he got in the batter's box, Pap turned to the new umpire and asked, "What's the count?"

The umpire's reply was, "It hit him in the mask, so it must have been a strike."

Pap said, "That's what I wanna hear," as the umpire held up his hands as 0 and 1.

Roe flew out for out number three, and we headed to our dugout on the 1st base side. Harry our manager now decided to speak up in an elevated tone. "Country, did you knock him out on purpose?"

"No sir!"

"Well, that's all I wanted to know."

Pap heard Harry and yelled, "Don't blame the kid, Harry. I called it, he did just fine. Country's doin' just fine."

Even though Harry raised his voice to me (elevated vocal sounds are quite common in sports) and put on his badass performance, he was still on my side. Hell, I was 5-0, soon to be 6-0, and this was just in the bottom of the fourth inning.

In the top of the 5th when we were up hitting, we could see the flickering red lights of an ambulance off the corner of the left field wall. Somebody yelled out from the bench, "Yeah baby, don't 'F' with Country!"

It reverberated through this old concrete pillbox of a dugout. All my games seemed to be close, but my guys always gave me enough to get over the hump. I eventually finished the game out. Complete games are like getting a mini rush, and to top it off this was my best game. I threw a one-hit shutout.

But, here's the bad part of the whole deal. The next morning, we had a 9:30 am flight to Des Moines, Iowa. George and I were rooming together, and we were at the Indy Inn. We were supposed to have a six o'clock wake up but the phone rang at 5:30.

I picked it up, and on the other line a voice said, "Country, this is Harry. You got a pen and paper?"

"No, let me look." I felt around in the dark and found an Indy Inn pad and pen.

"I want you to call the umpire from last night and apologize to him before we board the plane," Harry said. "Here's his name and here's the hospital number. You call him and apologize."

"Are you shittin' me (a common baseball term)!?" But Harry had already hung up.

George was half asleep, and he rolled over and asked, "Was that Harry?"

I nodded and told George what he wanted me to do. George's response was the same as mine, "Are you shittin' me (a common baseball term)?"

The bus to the airport was leaving at 6:45, and now it was 5:45. I hopped on the horn and called up the hospital. I knew what the chain of command would be because my Mom was an RN. I was shootin' for the head nurse on the floor, hoping I could pull this off. I got through and really had some explaining to do. The nurse told me the patient was sleeping.

"Can you just put the phone up to his ear...please? It won't take me but 30 seconds, I promise."

This nurse was cool about it after I thoroughly explained the situation. I could have gotten Nurse Ratchet but the Man Upstairs was with me. She said to call back around 8:30am, so I promised I would and hung up.

Now I had some breathing room. I went downstairs, got on the bus and made sure I had a quarter to make the call from the airport. We got to the airport, got in line and put our bags on the cart to be checked in. We had an hour to kill before we boarded, so we grabbed breakfast on the run, which was standard procedure.

Finally, 8:30 rolled around. George had spread the word about Harry waking us up and about me going to make this call. Most of the team was pretty pissed at Harry for making me make this ridiculous call. They all watched as I made my way to the telephone booth, grasping that quarter and pushing it into the slot.

I got through to the hospital and got connected to the nice nurse I spoke with earlier. She informed me he was awake, and said she was going to get another nurse to put the phone up to his ear. I was on the fast track. After a long minute, a voice finally said, "Ok Mark, you can talk."

Finally, I was going to talk to George the umpire.

"George? This is Mark Littell, huh, Mark Littell here...George, sorry I drilled you, bye." I hung up quick as I could after that. Glad to get outta that phone booth.

I did my deed and it only took me ten seconds and six words to get it out. Harry saw me come out of the phone booth, and he asked, "Did you get ahold of him and apologize?"

"You bet! Done deal," I said.

"Hell of a game you threw last night," he said, and then he walked away.

The things you do to win a game. Life's not always a bitch but you gotta go for that gusto. Even though we were still a nuisance and immature, the team started to include us younger guys. We were performing as good if not better than most, and I guess they were tired of giving us shit. We were there to stay or move up. I can truly say this: George and I would always be a nuisance and immature both on and off the field...but we had a blast.

❝ Baseball is the very symbol, the outward and visible expression of the drive and push and rush and struggle of the raging, tearing, booming nineteenth century.

- Mark Twain

KANSAS CITY ROYALS
BEATING THE ODDS

Playing professional baseball, for whatever team, is a great place to be. But, yes sir, you can bet the deck is stacked against you, with lots of unforeseen obstacles that pop up out of the blue. In my case, moving up to get a varsity spot with the Kansas City Royals was a rough road. As I said before, I made the team against the wishes of Farm Director Lou Gorman, but they sent me north to AAA Omaha. Lou felt I should have gone to AA Jacksonville, but gave me his blessings and off I went. By June 9th, I had 9 wins under my belt with 1 loss. Yes, I was on the top of the heap in the American Association. Since I didn't go to big league camp, there were some administrative guidelines in place and there was a chance that the Royals would have lost me to another club had they not called me up. I kinda blindsided the Royals by coming on this fast.

I got called up and made my debut on June 14th in Baltimore. I rode through 6.1 innings, while giving up 1 run. Fran Healy caught me that night and I did alright but we ended up taking a loss. I came out without a decision about where I should go next.

We went to Cleveland and played a four-game weekend series before flying back to Kansas City late Sunday night. They really didn't know what to do with me at this point, so they just told me to get a cab and go to the Muehlebach Hotel where they had a reservation and a room waiting for me. Elvis and the Beatles stayed here so I figured I must have been walkin' into a high cotton kinda place.

I ate lunch then took a cab out early to check out the baseball scene. Hell yes, I didn't have anything better to do and I was pitching that night so I decided I had better get my ass in order. Driving up to Kauffman

Stadium was impressive, it was brand spankin' new and everything looked to be in order.

The funny thing is, I had played in Kansas City before, back before this brand new stadium was built. In fact, I was the only minor league player to play in both Municipal Stadium and Kauffman Stadium.

As I pulled up to the new stadium, I couldn't help thinking about that first visit to Kansas City. It was hard to believe that, just last year, in 1972, I was playing in an exhibition game in the old Municipal Stadium. I got there early that morning to soak it up and take it all in. Those new ballparks are fancy and state of the art, but the old ballparks were full of history. I remember walking on the field to check out the pitching mound (a longtime tradition of mine), and while I was out there I noticed how pretty the grass looked. Somebody had spent some time on this piece of real estate. I started coasting across the grass thinking, *"holy shit I got the stadium all to myself"*…or so I thought.

As I approached the first base line, this loud voice started yelling at me. I knew it wasn't GOD, but it still scared the crap out of me. Then I realized the voice was yelling at me to get the hell off my grass. Again he said, "Get off my grass!"

I put the brakes on and saw this little sawed-off shit of a guy with a big voice strutting toward me. I sized him up as he got closer and I thought, *"this dude better know 'Kung Fu', I fight dirty."*

He got ten feet from me and said, "Whataya think of the grass?"

I paused and said, "It's great."

"Don't screw with my field," he said, and in the same breath he added, "You're Mark Littell?"

I nodded.

"Go out and check the mound out, you'll like it. I'm George Toma."

I snickered, and we shook hands. I didn't realize until later that I was shaking hands with one of the best, if not the best, grounds keeper in the country. Toma was very particular and sensitive about his grass and the field surface. The grass was crisscrossed perfectly and the mound was tight but not too tight.

When I arrived at Kauffman stadium a year later, I wondered if the grass would be just as good. I made it through the all-glass front doors and asked the meet and greet lady, "How do I get down to the players' locker room?"

She pointed to the wall with the doors and said, "Take the elevator down one level. Are you goin' to the home or visitors locker room?"

I said, "I'm wearin' blue!"

She smiled and said, "Then you will want to go to your right."

I made it down to the clubhouse and had to pinch myself. I was kinda standin' there gawking at what was just a hell-of-a joint to hang out in. One of the clubhouse attendants came over and asked, "Are you Mark Littell?"

"You bet!"

"Let me show you to your locker."

Well I'll be damned; they had everything all sorted out. I was early but there were a couple of other players that had come in early as well. I got halfway dressed and decided to check out the rest of this pad. I went back to the equipment room where the head clubhouse man, Al Zych, was busy getting things in order. We chewed the fat for a couple of minutes and he said, "Hey Country, did you sign the balls that were laying out on the spread table?"

"No, didn't really pay attention to any balls."

Well Al educated me and said, "Yeah you gotta sign the balls."

I walked back out and found the table with the balls. Pens lay there waiting for everyone's "John Hancock" to be plastered on four boxes of balls. When I was in Rookie ball, A-Ball, and the two months I spent in AAA, I had signed maybe four baseballs. So I was real excited to get my hands on them.

I was the first one to sign these 48 balls. I sized up the baseball and saw "OFFICIAL BALL" written on one side. The next line underneath read, "AMERICAN LEAGUE," and then under that, "Joseph E. Cronin PRES." all stamped in blue. I spun the ball a half turn and I thought, *"Now, here's a nice area that looks easy to scribble on."* I would soon find out that this was what they called the "sweet spot." I signed all 48 and took my time to make sure this first go around was a good one.

Well hell, I found out within a matter of twenty minutes that I had stepped outta bounds a little on this one. This area of the ball was reserved for the manager, Jack McKeon. I went back to my locker and paid little attention to the other players who walked up to the table snickering. They didn't sign the balls, they just spread the word that this "Country Boy" was more than a little raw; he might even be a Hick. They tried to keep the secret, but eventually it spread to the coaches.

I was over in my locker thinking about getting my brain straight and calming myself down for the game that night. To cut to the chase, Jack came out of his office dressed down, smokin' this big fat cigar and wearin' his bifocals. One hand was tucked inside his pants with the thumb on the outside. He looked like he had no worries as he very casually panned the locker room. One of the coaches said, "Jack, you need to go sign the balls."

"Yeah, I'll get to 'em in a minute."

Another coach spoke up and said, "No, Jack, you really need to go over and sign the balls."

Jack made it to the table, looked down, and picked up a ball, and then looked over his bifocals. With cigar in mouth, Jack chuckled and raised his voice, "Hey Country, you like signing the balls?"

At 30 feet away I said, "Sure."

"If you wanta keep signin' 'em don't put your name on the sweet spot!"

Yep, there was a big howl throughout the clubhouse. Jack walked back to his office puffin' away on that big cigar and shakin' his head as he mumbled, "Are you shittin' me?" (a common baseball term). Immediately the clubhouse guys brought in two ball bags and the 48 signed pearls disappeared. I figured these balls were goina be hit around during batting practice with "Mark Littell" scribbled on the sweet spot.

So much for mistake number one, but mistake number two would take a greater toll. That night I started against the Oakland A's, who were well stacked. They would dominate the American League Western Division from 1971 to 1975. Along the way they would win three World Series in this five-year span. The stadium was packed, them to top it all off there was no grass by George Toma. It was now this hot-rod turf put out by 3M. I got hammered and after 1.1 innings they threw up 4 runs. The stadium was packed, and all of a sudden I was on the tail end of a boar hog suckin' hind tit. In Kansas City I was now at the bottom of the pile. I would pitch two more times in the next twenty-three days, then go back to Omaha.

Before I went back to Omaha, Royals general manager Cedric Tallis called me upstairs for a talk.

"Mark, have a seat," he said when I entered his office. I guess he was into golf because he was practicing his putting at the time with one of these new-fangled, kick-the-ball-back gig-a-ma-dos. He told me to not let my guard down when I returned to Omaha. "Stay after it and learn from your mistakes." Cedric looked up and made eye contact between his 50/50 putting ability. Like my Dad always said, if a guy doesn't look you in the eye—don't trust him.

Cedric gave me a nice pep talk then said, "I'm going to leave you at the major league minimum salary." Back then this was $15,000. "You were an unexpected bright spot for the Royals," he added.

"Gee thanks, Mr.Tallis," I said, but what I wanted to say was, "Holy shit!" I was now making double of Gideon High School teacher.

I drove back to Omaha and as I was walking into Rosenblatt Stadium, pitcher Al Fitzmorris was walking out to catch a flight to Kansas City where he would take my spot. Al said, "Have a good time." Right. Clubhouse talk just went out to the parking lot. I was back to reality.

I finished out Omaha then went back to Kansas City in the September call-up. There was a lot of hoopla going on about the Royals having a chance to dislodge the Oakland A's (slim chance). But it would not be in the cards and we would finish at 7 games out.

Around this time, the Winter Ball conversation came up in the locker room as Latino General Managers were making their way around the clubhouse talking to prospective players. Places like Dominican Republic, Puerto Rico, and Venezuela were well represented and all were known to have good piña coladas. With less than a week to go, a couple of coaches had mentioned Winter Ball to me, but I had no idea who to talk to or what to say about nailing down a spot.

After batting practice, most of the players were trying to hone in on getting the job done between lines. That meant trying to slow that brain down. There was less than an hour before the game and it was chill time in the clubhouse when three representatives from Venezuela with the La Guaira Sharks had me cornered. Royals' manager Jack McKeon passed my locker as we were in mid-stream talks of why I should pitch in Venezuela. Jack stopped on a dime, backed up a couple steps and interjected, "He's going to play in Arecibo, Puerto Rico."

Just like that I went from being a potential Shark to an Arecibo Lobos (Wolves). Jack's words were crystal clear—I would drink piña coladas in Puerto Rico and pack on 75 more innings. I kinda liked that, "The Lone Wolf." I didn't know they had wolves in Puerto Rico.

After pitching in Puerto Rico, I got back to the States in mid-January where I would have less than a month of down time before reporting to big league camp in Fort Myers. I figured 27 innings in spring training, 179 innings in AAA, 38 in the Show, and 75 innings with the Lobos, was a good amount of innings to pack on in an eleven-month period. Yeah, I came in with 319 innings…isn't that great. Well, my arm didn't exactly feel so hot. I went into big league camp with a sore elbow. Maybe I needed more rest, because I went out on the first cut, back to Sarasota.

In a nutshell, I made it through spring training. It wasn't pretty and I made it through four games in Omaha before being shut down in May. I cried Uncle. By October they found out I would need surgery. It was an outside orthopedic surgeon Doctor Wiley Hutchins from Campbell's Clinic in Memphis who finally figured it out. They took a picture of my elbow, then after a short wait Doctor Hutchins came to talk to me. He held the X-Ray up to the window while takin' a drag off his cigarette. "Well looky here, I'll be damned,

Mark you've got a bone spur!" Three days later I
had surgery.

For the most part, when I started the season in
Omaha the injury kept getting worse. For the longest
time they thought it was in my head—a big BS to that.
After three cortisone shots over a four-month period,
along with anxiety stacked to the ceiling, I finally had
peace of mind. I wanted 1974 to disappear.

I had my surgery, my Mom helped with my rehab,
and I came back smoking. I even had a smile on my
face. In two and a half months I was better than ever—
what a turn around.

Me, deep in thought.

KANSAS CITY ROYALS

THE ROSTER

I went into big league camp in 1975 and expected to get cut on the first go. I went down on the second go around, but wasn't really pissed. Hell, I had missed a year. I got off to a slow start in Omaha but finished 13-6 before being called up in late August. But there was a new sheriff in town. Whitey Herzog had taken over the helm as manager and things changed. The chemistry was different. He took calculated chances and expected you to hold up to your end of the deal. I finished out 1975 in Kansas City. This time, I took a needed break from baseball. I needed a blow, but started working out six weeks before spring training.

I headed down to Fort Myers ready, but spring training was shortened because of an Owner's Lockout from March 1st through March 17th. This could have hurt guys like me who were borderline to break with the team to start the season. . I was focused on what spring training we had left. I was also semi-pissed off, which definitely gave me an edge. I threw 11 innings in spring training, but I dominated this time. With two days left in camp, I went over to Whitey who was toolin' around the outfield and asked him if I was goin' north with the team. He didn't hesitate and said, "Yes, you are, Country."

He gave me that amusing shit-eatin' grin of his as he spit out a nice stream of tobacco out to seal the deal. I proceeded to chase down a fly ball that came my way.

Not only was 1976 our Bi-Centennial year for the good ole USA, but it was a banner year for the Royals as well. The Royals finally dislodged the commanding Oakland A's, who dominated from 1971 to 1975.

Charlie O'Finley's (of Charlie O) Oakland A's had players that could put the bat on the ball, lay out frozen ropes, with an occasional long ball. Reggie Jackson would walk into the batter's box, and he liked to keep things clean. They had a lot of grit on the field as well: Bert Campaneris at shortstop, Joe Rudi in center, "Captain" Sal Bando at third base wasn't a bad defense either. Ray Fosse and Gene Tenace would keep the pitchers in line—both were "Little Generals," no bullshit kinda dudes. The pitching arsenal had guys like "Catfish" Hunter, Vida Blue, "Blue Moon" Odom, and Ken Holtzman to name a few. They were more than capable to toe the rubber and give you seven strong, if not the occasional nine innings, of electrifying shit that always seemed to find a home on either corner of the plate. With free agency now coming into play the mainstay of their 76 starting pitchers were Vida Blue and Mike Torrez.

Of course, Rollie Fingers was down in the bullpen digging into the mustache wax. He had to keep those handlebars that reached out to each ear lobe looking sharp for the camera. Rollie was not a pretty boy; he could get pissed off and close out a game in under three minutes. This team still had a lot of grit. They didn't need Dick Williams—matter of fact he left after winning the '73 World Series because he and Charlie

O had a few rounds about Charlie managing through the media. Alvin Dark came on as "Alvin Of Light" as they repeated and landed another World Series. Hell, they didn't need a manager, all the players had to do was write out the line-up themselves and if they were in a close game in late innings, just duke it out in the dugout to see who would make the call. Kinda like Willie Mays saying, "You don't need a 3rd base coach if you can play the game. The balls in front of you—get a read on it and hold or go." Playing baseball is not for a dumbass—it's a simple game but it takes a lot of drive and a whole bunch of other buzzwords to get the job done. First you gotta know yourself, second you gotta find out what your opposition can do. Then you gotta go out and play like your pants are on fire.

And that's exactly what the Royals did that special year of 1976. This would be the first time that the Royals would win their division and go into the Playoffs. I talked about the Oakland A's being a very solid team…well, so were the Royals. Hal McRae, who was part of Cincinnati's early "Big Red Machine," brought a big spark to the Royals. . Not only could he hit and play the field, but he also knew how to cut a second baseman or shortstop in half when breaking up a double play. Amos Otis, who came from the Mets, made it look easy in center field, plus he could hit in the clutch. Al Cowens who had a plus arm from right field would get you off the field and in attack mode at the plate. John Mayberry could pick it at first and drop some heads on a ball fast. Upcoming Frank White took over second and secured the right side of the field. Fifteen-year veteran Cookie Rojas, a Cuban player, filled in but could salsa and merengue well when turning a double play—nice hip action and a firm throw kept him on the field.

Of course, George Brett held down third base. Yep, Georgie could hit, field, and get the ball across the diamond. It was evident that George had learned a few tricks from Hal McRae on breaking up a double play. Those two were the dynamic duo; they were both Batman and Robin at getting those extra bases anytime they got a chance. To those opposing second basemen and the occasional shortstop that straddled second base when they came rollin' through, I just hope you guys didn't suffer too much pain in your later years.

Buck Martinez, Bob Stinson, and John Wathan kept the pitchers in line. Our pitching staff was a mix of youth and veterans. At the time it was made up of no-name guys who fell into the right crack. Dennis Leonard gave you innings and had some nasty shit. Paul Splittorff was a mainstay while adding and subtracting to keep us in the game. Al Fitzmorris went to the mound and put in over 200 innings even though his games took forever. When "Fitz" pitched we should have taken down a picnic basket—we really had to put a lot of extra shit into the bullpen bag.

Before becoming a Royal, tall and lanky Andy Hassler had lost 17 games in a row. Still, he was a good fit. When we took a 2-1 one lead in Cleveland, I came in and nailed down a save and a very much sought after win for Andy. When I entered the clubhouse, his arm was soaking in a tub of ice with a bottle of Champagne stickin' up with the cork popped. "Wanna glass?" he asked me. "Let's just spread the wealth."

Doug Bird stepped up to do some starting, 197 innings worth. You might say he made the most out of his starts. Both "Birdy" and Marty Pattin could start or relieve—both had time between the lines and it paid off. Steve Mingori was what you might say would be one of the first lefty specialists. He kept the bullpen loose with timely words of wisdom while constantly smoothin' out his mustache. Tom Poquette patrolled the outfield well and ended up hitting .302. He split time with Jim "Wolfman" Wohlford. Wolfman, who made the statement that 90% of the game is half mental, was all there. When asked if he could hit, Wolfman would look at you and say, "I can hit

anybody who throws me a fastball, a-n-y-b-o-d-y."
Unfortunately, he got a few breakin' balls that kept his
ass in line.

Veteran Dave Nelson knew the game well and
when he wasn't filling in pinch hitting or DH'ing
(designated hitter) he was talkin' over strategy with
Whitey. Davey was probably the first bench coach (not
knowing it) before the teams instated this new position
and title. This could be a good and not-so-good
position in many ways—according to the moment,
or win-loss record. If you were winning, the manager
might throw out the bench coach's name for bringing
up a quick thought in the heat of the battle. On the
other hand, if you were losing the manager could
blame it on the bench coach, behind closed doors of
course. Another scenario was if the manager never
brought your name into the mix and he got fired, you
would probably become the interim manager, but you
only held that position until the end of the season, or
until the bean counters found a fit.

Freddie Patek is why the little guy has hope. Yep,
Freddie was every bit of 5'4". He was primed in Seguin,
Texas and started pumpin' rockets across the infield
as a Big League shortstop with the Pittsburg Pirates
in 1968. He came to the Royals in a trade in 1971.
All pitchers of Royalty were blessed to have Freddie

behind us pluggin' up the hole on the left side of the field as well as up the middle. He had nice range. Whitey Herzog ranked Patek as the best artificial turf shortstop he ever managed, putting him ahead of Ozzie Smith. I pitched when they were both in the field and would have to say the baseball gods were in my corner. Our first baseman "Big John" Mayberry would just shake his head in the dugout after Freddie hit a homerun. With that big chuckle of a smile on his face, his follow up line was, "Freddie isn't goina be worth a shit for at least ten more at bats." Although to Freddy's credit he hammered out 3 homeruns in a game when playing for the California Angels. For being the "little big man" in the Big Leagues, he stuck around and played 14 years in the show. Not bad, Freddy.

I'm sure broadcaster Denny Matthews, who has been with Royals since inception, was having a blast with sidekick Fred White up in the booth. Every once in a while, if you looked up into the netting that ran from the backstop to that long line of media boxes, you would notice a paper plane gliding downward, with a few stuck into the lines of meshwork. I used to wonder if that plane signified a big hit or if one of these two misfits of baseball data had started their downward spiral of the twisted tongue. Had they turned the fact sheet into a paper concorde? Neither one was ever at a loss for words. In 2018, Denny Matthews will have 50 years of baseball in the booth. What a run. Congratulations Denny for giving Kansas City a class act.

I had a banner year in 1976 except for one pitch against the Yankees that still bothers me to this day. I still have people rib me about the "Blast in the Bronx." Hell, not too many folks know this but the next year was interesting because for some unbelievable reason in '77 we opened up at home with the Yankees. But more on that later.

We were all in it together, and remember, we were around each other a hell of a lot. Some would stay and become a franchise player like George Brett, some would be traded into the system, a few would be traded out, some came through the minor league system, and then some would be on their way out, their last round up. Even though the years may have gone by before we might meet again, there was a general tendency to gravitate together and pick up where we left off.

Kansas City Royals – The Roster

MISTAKE BY THE LAKE

GRANNY GETS COLD-COCKED

The year was 1977. The Kansas City Royals would win 102 games that year to claim the American League West pennant. We were on the road and playing a three-game set against Cleveland. The drawback was that we were in dismal Cleveland.

I'd been to Cleveland twice before, both in 1973. The first time was after my Baltimore debut. Cleveland was a pit stop where I spent three days in the hotel room, the hotel restaurant, and the ballpark. Like most rookies, I wore out my welcome after being lit up one too many times and was sent back down to hone my skills. I saw nothing else of Cleveland until a few months later, when I was recalled August 27th after a banner year in AAA Omaha. I'd finished 16-6 to claim the Allie Reynolds Award for Pitcher of the Year. I was to meet the team on the road in Cleveland, Ohio, of all places. This was known as a September call-up. I was excited about the call-up, but on the other hand I had heard some depressing stories about this city of doom. On this second go around in Cleveland, I was more relaxed and wanted to see more of this city setting on Lake Erie. Who knows, maybe it was the Florida orange belt of the north. But I would judge for myself.

Outside the Cleveland airport I jumped in a cab. The cabby loaded me up and asked, "Where you going?"

"Downtown to the Hollenden House," I replied.

We started moving steady through bits and pieces of small traffic. I said, "Cabby, there was an overcast sky at the airport."

"That wasn't an overcast sky," he said. "That's from those smoke stacks that blow up from the river. When the wind moves just right it covers the airport."

"No shit." I was twenty years old and still had soybeans and cotton comin' outta my pockets.

The guy said, "You from the South?"

"No shit," I thought, *"what gave that away?"*

"Yeah, I grew up on a soybean and cotton farm below the Mason Dixon Line, just north of Memphis. A little different than Cleveland. So cabby, what's so hot about Cleveland?

We were driving over this bridge into town, when he said, "Down there is the Cuyahoga River. Every once in a while it'll catch on fire."

"Fishin's not too good, huh?"

"Right now they haven't got any fish anywhere near those big factory pipes. You see those pipes don't you? It just keeps dumping, puttin' all kinds a shit in the river."

"No catfish swimming around even, huh … you mean bottom suckers can't even survive?"

Cabby said, "Nope, nothing really goin' on down there."

I said, "That sucks." I could just see myself goin' down to fish in the river and puttin' a worm on the hook then laying it down in the water for thirty seconds. I'd bring it back to the top and see that this worm is now white and solidified and stuck to the hook … yep, my kind of place.

Right then and there I knew nothin' good would ever happen in Cleveland. Whether it be at home or in the river city of flames, a stigma fell over me. I hardly ever threw well against Cleveland. Even if I had won the Cy Young award, I doubt that they would have given me the keys to the city. This cabby must have put a hex on me.

Clevelanders Say Go Indians

In 1914, new owner Charles Somers took over the helm of the Cleveland team and with it, a new team name. The previously named Cleveland Naps were named after a player/manager, and this tag was kept for a few years. Naps Lajoie was a fan favorite, but I can only imagine what the press would do to you on the sports page with a name like that. Naps in the field would not be a good start. So, Mr. Somers asked the local writers to come up with a name. They decided on a caricature of an Indian called Chief Wahoo. So the name Cleveland Indians was in place, and down the road when team mascots came into play in the 1970's, their lucky charm would be called "Slider." An Indian named Slider … I kinda like "Whamp Em" better.

Fast Forward Back To 1977

Cleveland Municipal Stadium was built in 1932; it was humongous and held 78,000. Beer night could be an absolute disaster, a giveaway night could become a tragedy, and a t-shirt night mixed with beer could be transformed into a nocturnal wet t-shirt contest.

On July 3rd, we were in town for the last game of the series, and they had one of those "give away nights." If you had a coupon you were in the running for a car, with fireworks to follow. Cleveland would be on the road the next day so the fireworks and the "give aways" were starting to add up. Yep, it was jam packed with 54,690 "Clevelanders"— this would be their largest regular season crowd and they were starting to get rowdy. Yes sir, it was going to be a real humdinger of a hoedown. Little did anyone know, it was going to be one of those double-edged sword nights.

Our bullpen hadn't gotten any real work in three or four days since the starters were doing their job. The rest of us were mostly left to observe. We needed to shake things up, so, Steve Mingori (Mingo) had this bright idea to spell out BULLPEN on the relievers' backs with white athletic tape. About six of us out of the bullpen got all doctored up in the dugout we then paraded in a single line across the infield to the bullpen just before the game. I just knew this was the kiss of death. . I thought back to 1973, on that September call up to Cleveland, and suddenly it made sense "the curse of the cabby." All of his energies would be pulled together to haunt myself, and many others who had the misfortune of visiting Cleveland. Yes, this would become hell night. But I didn't know it just yet.

We were laughing while going in stride to the pen. We had a front row seat to watch the overflow of a crowd hustling into their seats. When I got settled into the pen, I would usually set up shop trying to trade baseballs for hot dogs. To get a dog I would have to come forward to give a ball to a fan in exchange for a dog. I was a wheeler and dealer when it came down to food. It was one baseball for two quality dogs. No negotiating. I worked hard to get a decent dog; trading horsehide for pig lips sounded fair to me.

But here, it just would not work. First of all, the bullpen wall was so high up from the crowd, I felt that this would be a tough place to exchange and maneuver. In addition, the bullpen and dugout in this stadium were opposite lines from each other; the dugout was on the 3rd base side and the bullpen was on the 1st base side. Whitey Herzog the manager and Galen Cisco the pitching coach had a perfect view of the bullpen, and they would not think my trading balls for hotdogs was cool. I was throwing just all right anyway, no need to send a sideways message.

I couldn't stop thinking about a dog, but kept telling myself that we were in Cleveland. My mind started to rationalize the situation: I could get ptomaine poisoning, the fan I'm trading with could spit on my dog, I could get a cold dog with too much relish, not enough mustard, or worse, the dog could come back with catsup plastered all over that little puppy … just a very nasty scenario.

There was always a backup plan, though, and it was simple: the ball bag. Before going out the clubhouse door and heading down to the bullpen, somebody would yell out, "Who's got the bullpen bag?"

We didn't just have balls in this white canvas bag—we had a whole store. This carryall with straps had the things that counted, the things to give us that edge. Everybody loaded something different into this bag. At least six of our favorite candy bars, gum, chew, dip, pine tar, towels (carried through the straps), maybe a soda or Gatorade, and we were never without binoculars. All this was part of the commissary. We even threw in a few balls and maybe a rosin bag. The guy who used the rosin bag was usually OCD, and a real tool. We didn't have many of these guys hangin' around for long because they drove everybody nuts.

The bullpen at the Cleveland Stadium looked like a pillbox. When you walked through the gate of the chain link fence that was maybe forty inches high, it butted up to the warning track just past the 1st base line, not too far from the Cleveland dugout. There were two mounds with nice grass in between the plate area and the mounds. At the bottom of the stands, the first seats were elevated about 6 feet high, but as you looked up it graduated upwards to I gotta say 20 feet; it was way up there. Keep walking past the mounds and you walked into a bunker; this was an enclosure of probably 16' long by 7' high and 8' deep. This bunker was under the stands but was built in as part of the bullpen. It had two benches, a drinking fountain, and a phone. The worst part was you couldn't sneak up to the clubhouse for goodies because you were opposite the dugout. Hands down, it was the worst bullpen in the league. If I had lived in Cleveland in the 60's and the Cuban Missile Crisis was goina go down, I would have scaled the stadium walls and hunkered down in this bullpen bunker—it was solid.

When I played with the Royals, there were no bullpen coaches; we policed ourselves. And it worked...most of the time. But it didn't matter if we had had a bullpen coach on this particular night because, sure enough, we got into a pickle in a different sort of way.

Our starter was struggling some but had made it through six innings. We could see that the bullpen was going to be used and some of us would get some work, maybe even snag a game in the late innings. Our guys never quit.

In the meantime, there was plenty of hoopla going on in the stadium. One section was going nuts; someone had the magic number to that winning ticket. This wasn't a kiss the pig contest in Peoria, Illinois; this was people on edge with a baseball game going on as interim entertainment. Dennis "Leo" Leonard, was having another good season. He would be a

20-game winner this year but was hit and miss on this night. He ran into trouble in the seventh. We could see our pitching coach Galen Cisco making his way to the phone in the dugout and that's when we knew somebody was gonna get up. Doug "Birdy" Bird answered the phone. He listened for a couple of seconds, and then said, "Larry, get it going fast."

Larry hopped up and Bob "Scrap Iron" Stinson went down to the other end to catch.

For the whole game there were fans looking at us from the top of the pen with beers in hand, just hanging over the rail and yelling, "You suck! Can't join the rest of the real players on the big bench?"

F'ing morons.

Mingo yelled up and said, "You guys aren't going to waste any of that good beer by letting it fall on us are you?" In the bullpen we were always looking around for all sorts of potential objects to fall or better yet be thrown at us.

One of the fans responded by saying, "Don't worry, it's goina go down the right hole."

Larry came into the game with one out, and he also had one of those nights where the ball couldn't find the plate but when it did it complicated things; anything close to the plate fell in for a hit. Not long after Larry went into the game, another phone call came down. Birdy answered the phone again, and this time he said, "Country, get it going … quick."

Bob Stinson ran down to the other end as I fired off about seven pitches real fast in front of the rubber. I backed up to the rubber as he got down and I worked out of the stretch on the fast track. Whitey made his first trip to the mound with Larry to eat up time while I got loose. Whitey left the mound and let Larry get back to business to get us off the field. Now I could take a breather and started going pitch for pitch with Larry—he threw a pitch, I threw a pitch. I was close to being ready.

Remember, the bullpen we were in was somewhat tight. Even with a rope dropped down it would be hard to scale. It went straight up so it was practically impossible to throw a baseball out of this enclosure, especially with the command of any major league pitcher…right.

My last pitch in the bullpen decided to take its own course and would end up being my last pitch in this bunker. Working out of the stretch, I threw a fastball that flew out of my hand. It launched upward and went over and out of the bullpen. It cleared the top wall by about two feet. Yep, it was a loose fastball, a mini scud missile that would do some damage if it found a target.

The first thing that came into my head was "You're shittin' me" (a common baseball term).

Scrap Iron snickered as he pushed his mask up to the top of his head. "What happened?" he asked.

"Just lost it."

Everybody in the pen saw the ball go into the stands and we blew it off for about six or seven seconds. After seven seconds went by, war broke out. An incoming beer soared over the wall, and landed on the battlefield—I mean the pen. Then another, then another, and then a whole shower of shit rained down on us. We immediately took refuge in the bunker. Marty "Duck" Pattin said, "Holy shit, Country, you must've smoked somebody! They're all bent outta shape."

We couldn't see from where we were, but the whole right side of Municipal Stadium was up and ready to come over the wall.

Out on the field, Larry was in some trouble. Galen called down again and said, "What in the hell's going on down there?"

Birdy had the phone and said, "I think Country just drilled somebody."

All kinds of garbage flew into the pen. Even some hotdogs made their way down. At this point there were six-inch piles of all kinds of crap. You could barely see the grass in some places. I wouldn't want to be on the clean-up crew that night.

Galen asked Birdy, "Is Country ready?

"You ready?" Birdy asked me.

"Yeah." We were inside this bunker peeking out to see another irate fan hurl more garbage our way.

When Galen hung up, Whitey called down thirty seconds later. He never called down. "Put Airhead on."

I took the phone from Birdy.

Whitey said, "Air, what's going on down there?" Whitey had to elevate his voice as the war drums were starting to beat louder.

"Damn ball flew right outta my hand. I must have drilled someone up above, they're just all pissed off down here," I said.

"Here's what we're gotta do," Whitney said, as Buck Martinez was making the trip to the mound to eat up time. In other words, Buck and Larry were going to bullshit about what the hell was going on in the bullpen. "The safest place for you is right in the middle of the diamond."

"Yeah, he's right," I thought. *"That's why he makes those big ducats."* You just knew Whitey would have the answer.

Whitey called me "Airhead" a lot, and right then he said "Air, can you jump that bullpen fence and run to the mound?"

"You bet … no problem."

"Here's what I'm goina do. As soon as I touch the 3rd base line you make your move toward getting over the fence and making it to the mound. I'm not going to motion for you to come in, just get to the mound."

Yeah, he really couldn't motion for me. These pissed-off Clevelanders would have me run the gauntlet. That would definitely suck on my part. By the time I got to the mound I would be a relish tray.

He also said, "Don't go out the gate, you'll get hammered, so jump the fence."

"Gotcha." I was thinking this would be like maneuvering through a minefield.

Whitey came out of the dugout, and as soon as he hit the 3rd baseline I started to run through all the garbage, jump the fence, and make my way up to the mound. Whitey and Buck were there to greet me. Larry had made it back to the dugout. Whitey stood there in what I call his "commander's stance"— both hands in his pants with his thumbs hanging over the front of the belt, one leg forward and bent at the knee while he rested his weight on the back knee. He usually had some chew or gum in his mouth. Both he and Buck had big grins as Whitey said, "Air, what the hell's goin' on down there? From where we're sittin' it looks like a war zone?"

It was a repeat question. I guess both he and Buck wanted to get it from the horse's mouth. "Well shit, the ball just flew out of my hand kinda like there was goose shit on my fingers. It must have smoked somebody up there. Hell, the bullpen is just full-a shit, somebody's definitely pissed off."

They snickered and Whitey said, "Let's get outta of this inning."

Gotcha!

As I warmed up, the Clevelanders were starting to get up in arms. I couldn't help notice that the stands had now started to gain more repetition and consistency in their expressions of being, well, pissed off. The word had spread that there was an asshole on the mound. I'm just glad it wasn't "Chief Wahoo Tomahawk Night."

I got out of the inning and when I returned to the dugout, Galen said, "Hey, Country, you want another inning?"

"Damn right, skippy."

We failed to score and I went back to the mound in the eighth. The fans were still in an uproar as I hit pay dirt to warm up. They were loud and rowdy for the whole inning. When you get a ticket to a game, you come to have fun and get bent out of shape, gotta get away from the house and office to vent. They were venting all right. I got through the eighth, then headed up the tunnel to the clubhouse not wanting to watch the rest of the game. We would go on to lose, and I knew the shower that night would be good after all the drama and excitement.

I slid out of my uniform and got down to underwear and put a clean t-shirt on as I started poking around the spread. A lot of times we would eat the spread and not go out; we'd just go back to the hotel and watch TV or read, go to bed, whatever. They didn't bring out the main course until the game was over so I was just pickin' around on the bits and pieces as the two clubhouse guys were setting up. Larry and Dennis were up in the clubhouse along with Jim Colburn, one of our starting pitchers.

Jim came up to get the scoop. He asked me, "Hey, Country, what happened down in the bullpen? The fans started to get a little hostile, what the hell did you do man?"

Jim was a Rhodes Scholar and also a low level shit disturber. A good guy, and a very good pitcher who would later become the Los Angeles Dodgers pitching coach for a short time. He was trying to get more ammo to spread through the clubhouse after the game was over…obviously a California guy.

"Guess we'll find out. All I know is somebody probably got plastered," I replied.

That's when Bill Beck walked in. We were hitting in the top of the ninth and down three. Bill was our traveling secretary and a super guy. I had known Bill for a while. He did the radio play-by-play when I was in AAA Omaha. He walked up to me casually and said, "Country, how's it going?"

I said, "We're down a few so we gotta score, otherwise alright."

"Goina ask you a question?"

I said, "Shoot."

"Did you throw that baseball up in the stands on purpose?"

Everybody heard what he had said and watched as I turned and squared up to him. I gave him the hands-open gesture as I returned the answer with "Are you shittin' me?! (a common baseball term). The ball flew out of my hand. I was assuming somebody probably got smoked."

"Well, that's really all I wanted to know. You didn't do it on purpose, nobody pissed you off?"

For the last time, "NO."

Bill said, "Here's what happened. The ball you threw up into the stands leveled this older lady. It hit her in the head. They had to strap her on to a gurney and pull her out through the stands."

I can tell you this, when you're worn, concerned, and maybe a little flustered, the ole noggin is ripe for the ADD side to come out … at full blossom. You might call it "the bug in the mug." And boy was my mind buggin' out. My answer would come out like I took twelve years off my life. My shoulders dropped and my forehead looked like I had tin foil head, you know like you just smashed foil on your forehead with the palm of your hand … all crunched up.

My somber answer to Bill was, "You mean I knocked out a grandma?" I paused for three or four seconds then asked, "Do you think I should sign a ball for her?"

They weren't laughing – they were *howling*. Bill dropped his shoulders as he turned around with a direct 180. His head went down and he shook it slightly sideways with the 'no' motion as he walked out. I truly meant it in a good way, but well, it just kinda came out wrong.

I don't know which one of the guys said it but someone commented, "Yeah, Country, you did her in, you co-cocked granny, way to go." My vision was this older lady just sitting there watching the game and then a kamikaze baseball smoked her in the side of the head. Then she fell over sideways into her grandson's lap. Oh boy.

The game ended. It was low key in the clubhouse after we took a 6-3 loss but the ball that knocked out granny was the buzz of the night. The crowd was quiet now; all we could hear was the muffled sound of fireworks going off … just a bunch of low Ooh's and Ah's. I knew granny and the fish of the Cuyahoga were sleeping well that night.

THE BIG BANG ...
NOT A THEORY

It's About Time!
Yanks in Series

Chris Chambliss HR Ends 12-Year Drought

(*The Daily News*, Oct. 15, 1976)

A home run as dramatic as the one
Bobby Thomson hit 25 years ago this month
touched off a victory demonstration last night
reminiscent of Shea Stadium of 1969 and have
the Yankees a sudden death 7-6 victory over
the Royals and their first American League
championship in 12 years.

Chambliss connected on the first pitch of the last of the ninth inning and drove it over the blue fence in rightfield and, as the ball disappeared, the Yankees had won their 30th AL pennant.

Chambliss remained at home plate, watching the ball head for the fence. When it was gone, he threw his arms in the air in celebration and danced around the bases. His teammates were on the field and, before Chambliss could reach second base, thousand of young fans were swarming on the field, trying to get at Chambliss. He pushed and bulled his way through the crowd, but he never touched third and he still hasn't touched home.

Chambless tried, but by the time he reached home plate, there was no home plate. It had been carried off as a souvenir by some urchin and is probably in a Bronx apartment this morning. If necessary Chris will make a house call.

Brett connects in 8th

The blast by Chambliss came against Mark Littell and broke up a game that the Yankees seemed to have had under wraps until George Brett crashed a three-run homer in the eighth to tie it at 6-6 and set up Chambliss' dramatic shot.

The clock in rightfield said 11:43 and the centerfield scoreboard flashed the news: "Yankees, 1976 American League champions."

Thousands of fans who have waited so long for a return to the glory days celebrated wildly, even destructively. They climbed on the screen behind home plate, bouncing on it and dangling from it perilously. They shouted and screamed for more than 15 minutes. And they covered every inch of the field, picking up everything that didn't move for souvenirs of this exciting and historic moment in baseball history.

They were delirious. They were ecstatic. Their beloved Yankees were going to the World Series again, scheduled to meet the Reds in Cincinnati in the first game tomorrow.

Chambliss' Take

Looking back to the 1976 League Championship series against the Kansas City Royals is always a pleasure for me, for obvious reasons. My game-winning home run in the bottom of the ninth put the New York Yankees in the World Series for the first time since the early 60's. It was the first year playing in Yankee Stadium after a three-year renovation project. Every game was full of action as the series played out much the same as our games during the regular season.

Our rivalry with the Royals had become as strong as the Yankees vs. Red Sox. The Royals were strong, with great pitching, defense, power and team speed and it all was displayed during the series. After numerous lead changes during the series, and especially in game 5, our 3-run lead was erased by George Brett's 3-run homerun off Grant Jackson late in the game. It set up the moment in the bottom of the ninth.

Mark and I had a long delay before that pitch was thrown since the fans had thrown all kinds of debris in the outfield. As the ground crew cleaned off the field, standing around while it was so cold was a challenge and added to the suspense.

I hit the first pitch a fastball high in the air to right field. It cleared the fence by only a few feet. My trip around the bases was thrilling and scary at the same time since Yankee fans charged onto the field. After falling to a knee at second base and pulling down my helmet to avoid it being taken, I somehow made my way into our dugout and clubhouse. But after being asked if I had touched home plate, I decided to put on a jacket and had two security cops take me back to home plate where I found that it was dug out and taken somewhere. I touch the area anyway and headed back to the clubhouse.

Our rivalry continued in the LCS in 1977 and 1978 and even later in the 1980's after I was traded away. It was a time in my career I will never forget.

- Chris Chambliss

This was a tough one for me, my teammates, and Kansas City. To this very day, I'm often reminded of the game-winning walk-off by Chris Chambliss in New York.

On October 15th, the 1976 American League Championship Series between the Kansas City Royals and the New York Yankees would be decided in the fifth and final game in Yankee Stadium. The Cincinnati Reds swept the Philadelphia Phillies for the National League Championship, and were headed to the World Series. I'm sure the Cincinnati "Big Red Machine" players were setting back watching the game to see if they would fly west or east for the big game.

Forty-five minutes before game time we were all getting ready in the clubhouse, layin' low and going through our own game plan. Whitey walked into the middle of the room and elevated his voice to say, "Listen up guys." Holy shit, what's on the "White Rat's" mind? Like I've said before and most players and coaches know, Whitey has maybe four club house meetings a year. Hum, this must be number four.

Of course Whitey was in his commander's stance, as he said, "Guys, real quick before we get goin'. After we pick up this win we'll be flyin' out early tomorrow morning to get over to Cincinnati. See you after the game." Now if that wasn't cool. Like I've said before and anybody who's ever played for Whitey knows, he was short and succinct with his clubhouse talks.

In the top of the eighth, George Brett tied it up at 6-6 with a three-run shot off Grant Jackson. After a bum call on Al Cowen's slide into second base, we took the field again. I'm anything but an excuse guy. There was no replay then, and there was no reason to argue the call, because each and every game has a different rhythm—or let's say "personality."

Anyway, as soon as we came out of the dugout and hit the field, the Yankee fans did too. There weren't any bodies on the field yet—but there were plenty of bottles, batteries, and cups. One of the ballplayers said he kicked at a condom (still in its wrapper). As the Yankee ground crew started picking up the garbage, the Yankee sound system boomed. If you have ever been in Yankee Stadium, then you can imagine the voice of Bob Sheppard, calmly trying to get the Yankee fans in line.

Meanwhile our catcher, Buck Martinez, was squatting behind the plate so I could get loose (standard procedure). After about my fourth warm-up pitch, I caught a glimpse of our outfielders in a stationary stance. Their uniform numbers faced me, and they stood with their arms folded or their gloves on their hips, looking to see what might come out of the stands next. Clearly, the game had to wait. The players didn't want to get hammered by whatever might come their way. The infield stopped, and Buck stood up while I held my ground on the mound. There were low-hanging clouds moving from the third base side toward right field, it was cold. I turned back to face the plate, looked at Buck for a couple of seconds, and then motioned him towards me.

He came out to the mound, and as soon as he touched pay dirt I said, "Let's get the hell outta here."

"No," he said, "they're getting it. Let's just wait a minute."

In under a minute, the field was ready to go, and I threw a few more warm-ups. Roughly seven minutes after we had left the dugout, left-handed hitter Chris Chambliss stepped into the box. As he settled in, Buck threw down a sign, and I nodded in acknowledgment—we were on the same page. I wound up, and delivered a fastball up in the zone. Chambliss swung and connected. The ball went high in the air. With the wind blowing out to right, this was not good. The Yankee's short right-field porch could be a magnet for a left-handed hitter. Sure enough, the ball

went over, clearing the fence by less than three feet.
Hal "Mac" McRae was in right, and Al "A.C." Cowens
holding down center. They both told me later that
it barely went out, but that didn't make me feel any
better. They were absolutely great, trying to help me
pull myself together. But I just wanted it back.

The second it cleared the wall, the field of
Yankee Stadium flooded with people. The Bronx Zoo
stampeded this sacred turf. When I turned around and
looked into our dugout, our guys were starting to move
toward the runway. I dropped my head as people
made it to the mound before I even got to the grass.
As the crowd thickened, I just walked in a steady pace
toward the dugout. I made it down the steps into the
bottom of the dugout, and saw Freddie Patek sitting
on the bench with his head down. It wasn't until I got
to the runway that I finally escaped the commotion.
New York's finest more or less shuffled me into
the clubhouse—ready, I'm sure, to hit the field and
hammer a few heads. I heard the next day that they
had brought to bring out the horses. Police on horses
in close quarters couldn't have been fun for the locals.
I'm sure the Yankees owner George Steinbrenner
was working his way down to the clubhouse for the
celebration. Actor Cary Grant had followed him in to

pop the cork and raise the glass for the festivities. Well La-Dee-Dah.

As soon as I got to the clubhouse, leaving behind a sea of the dark uniforms and brass buttons, I headed directly for the showers. Hat, glove, uniform were all in place, I didn't have my jacket—it was left in the zoo. I stepped into the clubhouse and walked directly to the shower room and leaned into the back wall. I was beside myself. We had worked hard to be there, and I had just spoiled the whole damn season with one pitch. Whitey, pitching coach Galen Cisco, Amos "A.O." Otis and Dave Nelson were back there with me. I didn't know what to do or think. Then, after five minutes or so, I tried to rein myself in and act somewhat normal. I went back to my locker and calmly answered the questions from the reporters, took a shower, got dressed, boarded the team bus, and made it back to the Sheraton Hotel. A.O. and Davey helped me a lot—they all did.

When we had landed back in Kansas City the next day, we had several fans that had come out to meet us and give us their support. I really didn't want to look at anyone or talk to anybody—the whole thing was just a real downer. I became a couch potato and chilled.

The next day I decided to go down to the stadium and clean out and tidy up my locker. I said hi to the meet and greet lady then headed downstairs. There was the normal fan mail that was put into a box in the bottom of the locker but on top of my stool was a telegram. This was cool—I never had gotten too many telegrams. I picked it up and read the message: MY THOUGHTS ARE WITH YOU MARK I LOVE YOU. ETHEL BRETT 10/15/76

Yeah, I smiled as my eyes welled up. George's mom was at least in my corner.

The winter was tough as I tried to keep my head up. I hunted a hell of a lot. I ran into a few of the locals who gave their two-cents worth on how I let so many people down. Saw a waitress, waiter, and a workout guy at a gym get fired for giving me hell. On three separate occasions I aw a waitress, waiter, and a workout guy at a gym get fired for giving me hell. I was already on my way out the door as they got canned.

I actually think some folks didn't know what they were going to get when I returned to the mound. But they needn't have wondered. First of all, pitchers who close out games only have like a three to five I.Q. (generally speaking), so they're rarely in danger of overthinking a bad outing. And I was no exception.

Remember, I marked for DDT planes, so I had been well lubricated with all the toxins and concoctions that kill just about anything. (Southeast Missouri had to have been some kind of test ground to see how many kids would be born with six fingers.) Second, once I got around a baseball field I really did like to compete, that part was a blast. Third, I always liked to prove people wrong.

A husband and wife team out of Boston put the entire schedule for Major League Baseball together, three years in advance. And who would believe it? Of all things the strange things, our 1977 home opener was against none other than the Yankees. Déjà vu.

But before this, we opened on the road in Detroit for a normal three-game set. Around 46,807 people showed up to freeze their asses off at Tiger's Stadium. I came in and got a save in the first game. We also got a sweep. Nice start. We then returned home for our opener against the Yankees on April 11.

In this game, Paul "Split" Splittorff went the first nine, keeping us in a tie ballgame at four apiece. Nobody was budging—putting up a run was tough— but finally in the thirteenth, Big John Mayberry drove in Freddie Patek from second to give us a 5-4 win. And meanwhile, I had passed my own test, entering the game in the tenth and throwing four innings with good defense. I didn't give up a single hit, but of course I always had to throw out a couple of walks to make it interesting. Buck Martinez gunned down Mickey Rivers and Willie Randolph to stop any surge—way to go Buck.

During the '77 winter meetings in December, Buck and I were put into a trade for Cardinal Lefty pitcher Al Hrabosky, the "Mad Hungarian". Although Buck went north to Toronto in another transaction, I would go east to be a Cardinal and wear red. So 1978 would be a new but familiar territory. Coming into play in the National League was not as much of an adjustment as one would think. The hitters had never seen me and I wasn't afraid to challenge so all I had to do was to still try and mix in a strike. Hum Baby.

```
KC ROYALS

WU INFOMASTER    1-002610C289 10/15/76
ICS IPMKCKB KSC
 02004 (2-001163E289) PD 10-15 0123
TWX 9107712008 KC ROYALS
2133222522 NL TDRN ELSEGUNDO CA 100 10-15 0123A EST
MARK LITTEL, KANSAS CITY ROYALS DLR
KANSAS CITY MO
MY THOUGHTS ARE WITH YOU MARK I LOVE YOU
   ETHEL BRETT

0745 EST

KC ROYALS
```

*The telegram George Brett's mother
sent me after the Yankees game*

ST. LOUIS CARDINAL BASEBALL

TRADITION

At five years old, I watched my first baseball game on a black and white TV in Wardell, MO. The New York Yankees were playing the Detroit Tigers and I remember three names: Yogi Berra, Whitey Ford, and Al Kaline. It was "The Game of the Week"... well, the only game of the week. My Mom was pointing out these three guys over and over, and then she threw in this fourth guy named Mickey. Well, names like these just don't go away. Xbox wouldn't be around for another fifty years so I was glued into an antenna stuck on top of a box with black and white pictures that had lines going through 'em.

I liked what I saw and was settled for the moment. Pee Wee Reese and Dizzy Dean were doing the play-by-play and both kept you entertained. Both were different in their own way but had appealing redneck qualities Pee Wee with that sharp shootin' Kentucky tongue was there to keep his sidekick Dizzy the Arkansas country boy in line.

Even though I was now exposed to the outside world and game of baseball, I would soon find out that my team of choice would be the St. Louis Cardinals. We were in Cardinal Country and when we needed a break, we went north 180 miles to St. Louis to catch a game. We saw guys like Stan Musial being "Stan the Man", Julian Javier doing the some fast movin' salsa at second, Dick Groat knocking balls down at shortstop, Bill White scooping up everything at first, and Curt Flood just taking over centerfield, not bad. Then with the battery of Tim MacCarver behind the plate and Bob Gibson on the hill…yeah baby, what a team. I know the list goes on but from a very young age I always wanted to play baseball—just like those guys.

Other than the baseball games, we found amusement riding the streetcars in St. Louis. That was an absolute blast. The sounds, the smells, the ringing of the bell on the streetcar tellin' people to move it, left me with many diverse, distinct thoughts. Gaslight Square was a sight to see, and eatin' on "The Hill" where Garagiola and Berra grew up was very special. Hell, I was becoming a cultured country boy.

It was in St. Louis that I saw my first Big League game. It was at Sportsman's Park off of Grand Boulevard and Dodier Street. When you're a little guy and seeing people movin' and walkin' into this enormous, grand old park, you wonder if the walls could just talk. What a sight to see, these guys must be good. The reason I say this now is because a good portion of my life was spent in a professional park or on the field. There is an unwritten rule in baseball: "What is said on the field stays on the field." You can also add "in the clubhouse" as well. No wonder this place was so grand and old, it was built in 1881. There were numerous names changes and several rebuilds over the years to keep it tidy. It was added onto at different intervals, one time because of a fire. Baseball history at its best. This was a shared stadium occupied by the Browns and Cardinals for many years, since St. Louis couldn't support two teams.

But then the Cardinals won six World Series, and eventually the stadium was bought out by Anheuser-Busch in 1953. Well holy shit, I was born in 1953! It was now going to be a one-horse team town, but it was going to be a big horse, like a Clydesdale. August "Gussie" Busch bought the team and I can vouch that he not only loved beer and his Clydesdale horses, he also treasured his St. Louis Cardinal Baseball team.

Sportsman's Park held 30,611 people. When I saw my first professional game there in 1963, the Cardinals were playing the San Francisco Giants. The newspaper and other tabloids would read "Willie Mays and Company in Town." I remember sitting at the very top, nosebleed section. If I looked over my shoulder either left or right I got a great view of the city. Dad must have paid extra for these seats.

But I was glued in on the field, watching as much of the game as I could. Every play, every movement, was fascinating. My mother always kept a scorebook and would double down giving us the play-by-play. Early on we would be sitting (way up there) where we'd have to rubberneck around an I-beam to see the completed play. She really did follow the Cardinals, and was trying to explain why something was done, and why one guy moved to his left and the second baseman held his ground, and how Willie Mays could hit an opposite field homerun into the net off of Curt Simmons. "Because he's Willie Mays," said Mom.

That was my first Big League game and my first time in Sportsman's Park. On May 8th, 1966 the Cardinals moved to the new state-of-the-art Busch Stadium, and the scenery and setting were much different and accommodating. I was fourteen years old when I set foot in Busch stadium. The sight and smell of this massive arena grabbed me … what an impact. Hell, I didn't want to watch baseball. I wanted to play it. In my mind there was only one place to be: on this field.

It took a while, but it finally happened years later. At the winter meetings on Dec. 8th, 1977, both Buck Martinez and I were traded from the Kansas City Royals to the St. Louis Cardinals for Al Hrabosky. Buck was soon put into another trade, which sent him to Toronto, and I stayed in St. Louis. So, I was now a Cardinal and would get to see a very familiar town, with a new league and new players.

After the trade came around in the middle of January, I called up Bing Devine the general manager and let him know that I was coming through St. Louis on my way to the Bootheel. I wanted to meet him and make my way down to the clubhouse to just check out anything else that might get me settled into the St. Louis area. I parked and walked into Busch Stadium and a sign pointed me to the offices to the right. I walked in and saw the meet-n-greet lady and let her know that I was Mark Littell and had a meeting at 10:00 with Bing Devine.

She said, "Just a minute," and when she came back she asked me to follow her down the hall. I walked into Bing's office, we shook hands and I sat down. We did the small talk thing for about five minutes before he said, "Would you like to see the clubhouse?"

"Sure would."

We went down the stairs and, as I had thought, the clubhouse wasn't empty. I could see that there were two guys getting after it, packing, getting things ready to ship to the Cardinals spring training site in St. Petersburg, Florida. One was a young guy and the other just a hell of a lot older.

Bing called over the older guy and introduced him to me as Butch Yatkeman. He was a little guy, maybe 4'10 with white hair, very white skin and black-rimmed glasses. He came over doing the fast walk, kinda like the Olympic speed walkers, and then stopped fast looking up at Bing and me with both hands on the hips. I could tell this guy had tenure, so I would tread lightly.

Bing said, "Butch, this is Mark Littell one of our new pitchers."

Butch's response was, "So you're the country boy?"

"Yeah, nice to meet you Butch."

"Well, what number do you want, country boy?"

"I'll take number 17," I said.

All hell came out of Butch as he stepped closer to me. This little sawed-off shit said, "You dumb SOB that's Dizzy Dean's number! It's retired!"

So much for me treading lightly!

"And let me tell you something," he continued. "I'll see you come and I'll see you go. I've seen everybody come and I'll see everybody go and don't forget it."

My response was, "You got number 34?"

Butch said to Bing, "I like this guy" and he walked away. That was also the last time I heard him say, "I like this guy." Butch was a walking history book but my final conclusion was that somebody has to slip some

Prozac into this guy's water. I'll say it over and over again: don't ever piss off the clubhouse guy.

But I did wonder if some dementia had set in on this little fart. Butch had been around a while. He started as a batboy for the Cardinals in 1924—the Babe Ruth era. Having nine World Series rings pretty much stated he'd seen a few things happen. He was still kind of a sour puss. But true to his word, he did see me come and he did see me go.

One thing about walking into a big league clubhouse was that anybody was game. No matter how good you are, going into a Big League clubhouse can be a relentless territory. I couldn't believe that this clubhouse guy had beaten the players to the draw. We weren't even in spring training and this guy was already on my ass. Yeah baby, this was going to be one tough outfit that lived up to their name.

Retired heavy hitters like Bob Gibson, Tim MacCarver, Joe Torre, and Stan Musial might float through the clubhouse but we needed all the help we could get in my first year with the Cardinals. Vern Rapp, the manager, wanted me to go back to starting for some off-the-wall reason. He had remembered me dominating in AAA Omaha. Yeah Vern, just because I beat up on your Indianapolis team and the American

Association didn't mean I was going to coast through the National League.

The last two years I had mostly closed until I wore out my welcome with the Royals. It had been four years since I was a starting pitcher. At the time I was well armed with a 93-to-95mph fastball and an 87 mph slider that had depth, so that was kind of a plus. The kicker was I liked to take the mound under any circumstance, and as long as my arm was somewhat healthy I could dominate. In other words, I would fall under thrower rather than pitcher so the slider separated me some because I could throw it for more strikes than the fastball.

Yep, I fell under the category of a closer, 3 to 5 IQ included. Point me to the mound. I did start for two games before Ken "KB" Boyer replaced Vern. In '78, we had an ugly stick hit us early as we lost twelve games in a row, and you don't do that in St. Louis. Tar and feathers awaited someone and Vern was first in line. The first thing KB said to me was, "Country, you're going to close, you alright with that?"

You bet.

Redbird Baseball 1978-81

Lou Brock was simple and quiet but also driven. He stayed to himself but would listen and lead well. The younger guys, and even some of the veterans, watched what successful players did to quell any storm. Sometimes nothing said was best; we were professional but kept our eyes and ears open.

I remember telling Lou about watching him play in 1964 when I was 11 years old. I was 25 now and in a Cardinal clubhouse. "Hell, Lou that was 14 years ago!"

All Lou said was, "Ouch," with a smile and snicker.

Even as an older player, Lou looked and played the part well. He was a student of the game. Besides being an intense competitor, Brock was also very cerebral. When he heard that Maury Wills kept a little black book in which he noted pitcher idiosyncrasies, he asked Wills if he would share some of his notes. Not surprisingly, Wills was not eager to share the information he had painstakingly recorded to a player from an opposing team. So Brock went out and bought an 8-mm camera in late 1964 and began to record the league's pitchers to study their pickoff moves. Dodgers' pitcher Don Drysdale asked Brock one day what he was doing with the camera and he replied that he was taking home movies. "I don't want to be in your goddamn movies, Brock," Drysdale replied and true to his nature he threw at him the next time up.

I would have to say that Lou was one of the first to inadvertently take up visualization with the assistance of a camera. For all of you who are still reading this part about Lou Brock, I will give you three of his major accomplishments: He was inducted into the baseball Hall of Fame 1985; a 6-time All-Star ('67, '71, '72, '74, '75, '79); he broke Ty Cobbs all-time major league stealing record of 897, finished with 938. Don't know who Ty Cobb is? Look him up.

Bob Forsch who played third base in the minors was one of the mainstays as a starting pitcher. What a transition. The good thing with this scenario is that he could hit some but he ended up pitching fourteen years for the Cardinals. Consistent, steady, under control and all the accolades that come with this territory were in his corner. Bob was cool, but he was an low flying shit disturber. He'd get something started in the clubhouse or sound off or add on when something got started, then step back and snicker as others chimed in to keep someone in hot water. Bob Forsch could add and subtract and spot a fastball, flip a curveball in to keep you honest, and then throw you a dead fish to get the hitter out front for further frustration. In other words, he had a nice arsenal of pitches. Two no-hitters and 163 wins says you're livin' right in the baseball world. The baseball gods liked Bob as he finished with 16 years in the show.

Ted Simmons was beyond being very calm, cool, and collected about the whole hitting thing. We called him Ted, Teddy, or Simba because of his long mane of hair. Teddy was deadly at the plate and could leap onto a pitch that lurked in his zone. One of the best statements I've ever heard from a player was when I asked Teddy about an opposing starting pitcher. I saw Teddy sitting on the bottom of his locker in his shorts, t-shirt, and shower shoes. Teddy was contemplating his game plan as he took one of those long drags off his cigs as he so often did. In the 70's, tobacco was a vice for most of us including me, though mine came out of a can.

My question to Teddy was, "Hey, Teddy? Can you hit this guy starting tonight?"

Teddy looked up at me then looked down as he took another long drag off his cig. He squinted his eyes and calmly looked up at me and said, "I can hit anybody." That was it. And it was true; Teddy could hit anybody. He could also hold a pitching staff together and was a true student of the game. He was obsessed with every facet of the game, the moment, the beat, the rhythm of progression, the last pitch, and especially the last out. Teddy finished with 21 years in the show and needs to be in the Hall. He's still swingin' and going strong.

Pete Vuckovich would find a way to beat you. The plus about "Vuck" was that he had this underlying and calculated mean streak built into his persona, but it didn't really show up in his body language. It was a great feature to have as a competitor. To me this is a prerequisite—being a little cruel or uncaring can bring you into focus PDQ. Vuck was tough and would definitely fit in as an ultimate MMA fighter. In 1982, when Vuck was part of the big trade with Milwaukee, he claimed the Cy Young award for the American League. The Cardinals and Milwaukee would end up meeting in the '82 World Series as the Cardinals took the Series in game 7.

A LAWYER TAKES ME OUT OF A GAME

Chavez Ravine is just off of downtown Los Angeles. It's rich in history but better known for housing Dodger Stadium, a special place for me because my first National League win came here in 1978.

On my first trip to Dodger Stadium, I went out early to check out the field. This is a must for me. Spatial awareness is big on my list: getting to know the mound, the bullpen, the distance from the dugout to line, distance to the backstop, anything that could offset or be an asset to my game psyche. If I was familiar with the surroundings it made me feel more at home.

The whiff of Dodger dogs made its way down to the field, so that was a plus. My sniffer was honed into that scent. You could bet that I was goina be tradin' balls for dogs tonight. Since I was deaf in my right ear I couldn't hear for shit, but my nose was always on alert, like a German short hair tracking down a covey of quail. I would be open for business from the second through the fifth inning, and after downing a couple of dogs, everything would settle in by the time I got into the game, which would usually be anywhere from the seventh inning until "game over."

Since a lot of our players were from the west coast and it was a charter flight, most of the wives would make this trip. If you were unmarried and playing well, and getting a few hits, or mixing in a few outs as a pitcher, you could maybe negotiate to get your girlfriend on the flight west. Believe me, this didn't happen much, but we usually liked the scenery. Very few of our flights were passenger flights; we flew charter for convenience and it kept us out of trouble. Somebody would usually be about to have a bad game or would be in a slump, and then there were the occasional fans that took a seat right next to you on the plane and just can't hold it in any longer, "You guys suck!"

Yes, this would always draw attention and quite possibly get some guys dandered up. We just snickered and put the headphone set on and took the joyful ride west.

That night we were in the normal Dodger-Cardinal matchup. Cardinal announcers Jack Buck and Mike Shannon were in their spot calling the good, bad, and ugly and Vin Scully was of course anchored in his well broken in seat to call the Dodger's play by play. Bob Forsch was toeing the rubber for us as Rick Sutcliff took the mound for the Dodgers. "Forschie" was having a tough night as they scored 5 runs in 1.2 innings of work. In came my buddy Tom Bruno who gave up 3 runs, and then Will McEnaney gave up a run in an inning of work. Yes, Mac was one of the heroes in the '75 World Series when he pitched for Cincinnati's "Big Red Machine." He threw the last pitch to Boston's Carl Yastrzemski for the final out to take the Series.

The score stood at 9 to 1 after 5 innings. It was a mess of a game across the board. Let me say this, this is not the type of game you like to get into. Everybody on the other side is happy, happy, happy as they start to free swing. My job was to get outs but also make them feel a little uncomfortable. They knew well I could become conveniently wild and they might very well end up with a ball in their side or if it was close to the head their shoulders might hit the ground first before their feet got back down to earth. Yes, it could be an unhappy moment for the hitter, and to me it fell under the category of "Tough Shit." Baseball is such a great game.

I came into the game and started the 6th inning. I got two quick outs and then Bill Russell stepped into the box. I wasn't overly concerned about the Dodger lineup; I seemed to always throw well in Dodger Stadium yet when I was throwing well I would always like facing the big boppers rather than the line drive type hitters. The big boppers have the longer swings and are up there for one thing: to hit the ball out. If you're "ON" you got 'em, but if you make a mistake they hit a rocket. The next day you read about 'em spoiling what you thought might be an easy win. Then you've got the line-drive hitters, or flat bat. They have a controlled swing and generally take the ball up the middle. Once in a while you run into that "Punchin' Judy." These little farts are borderline OCD and generally flit in and out of the box like they got a bug up their ass. They're OFP (on their "Own F'ing Program") guys. This is the kind of guy that would wait you out and not swing until you threw that first strike. When you go to the bump they know your history, and my past said that this guy Littell could strike you out or give you a free ride to first with a walk. Which Littell were we going to see tonight? Would he challenge and pitch or make it interesting?

I threw a ball on the first pitch to Russell. The second pitch was on the barrel and he connected. A line drive shot back up the middle as it found my watermelon head. Actually, I saw the ball before it hit me, but a line drive straight back up the middle looks kinda like an aspirin tablet until it makes contact with your forehead. Yep, this ball found my noggin. It knocked my hat off but I was still standing, somehow. I remember the people rising outta their seats as I spun back around. I looked at Swish, and then back down at the mound and then looked up to try and find where this ball landed. Gary "Tempy" Templeton, our shortstop, was jogging over to me and said, "Country, what the hell? You alright, bro?"

I responded, "Where's my f'in hat?"

"Here it is, Country," Tempy said.

The crowd hadn't sat down yet; they were waiting for me to drop. This was why they bought tickets! To see some excitement, and maybe a little blood.

Gene "Geno" Gieselmann our trainer came walking out of the dugout and crossed the first base line. He was followed by our manager, KB. Lee Weyer, the home plate umpire, came walking up as well, so we had a pretty good crowd around the mound. I would later find out that during this part of the drama, Vin Scully was on the airwaves saying, "Littell has still not gone down!"

Before anybody said anything else, I asked Tempy where the ball landed.

He said, "It one hopped Tony out in center."

My response was, "Why the hell didn't he catch the SOB?"

Geno had a shit eatin' grin on his face and I know he was thinking *"You hard-headed SOB, why aren't you down?"* He said, "Country, what's going on?"

I said, "I think I can hear outta that other ear."

I've been deaf in my right ear since twelve years old. Believe me, everyone knew it because I would either say, "Huh," or keep on walking without even acknowledging you. The ball to the head didn't cure me, but it really should have.

Swish looked at me with that roving eye of his and said, "Country, shouldn't you be down?"

"Why hell no! Swish, all it did was knock my hat off."

Tempy chimed in again, "Country... that ball just knocked the ever livin' shit outta you."

KB got in his two cents, "Country, are you alright?"

Then it was my turn to ask a question. I said to the plate umpire, "Lee, you wanna ask me if I'm alright? I said I'm alright everybody. There are two outs, so all you guys get off the mound and we'll get this inning over with, I'm fine."

Geno asked, "You want to take a couple of warm-up pitches?"

Lee Weyer spoke up, "Yeah, take a couple throws."

In the meantime, this game was being broadcast back to St. Louis on KMOX where all the Cardinal fans were glued into Cardinal baseball. I guess there was an Anheuser-Busch legal eagle lawyer watching the game and for some reason he must have gotten concerned about me still being on the mound. I ended up throwing three pitches and they hit the mark with some pop and movement on the ball. On the third pitch, I turned to everybody who was still standing around the mound and said, "Why hell look at that, I'm throwing better now than before I got smoked."

There was some real time-lapse in all this hoopla but finally, everybody cleared the field and we were set to play ball. Everybody in the stands returned to their California kickback mode, relaxed and settling into their seats for some more baseball. I just know that during the downtime I had to have sold a few more beers and Dodger dogs for Dodgers Inc. Maybe they would send a few down to the pen the next night.

The next hitter stepped into the box and Lee Weyer motioned, "Play ball." With Russell on first, I stepped into the slot in front of the rubber and got the sign, then moved my hands level with my chest as I came to set, then took a peek at first. Before I could get in the pitch, Lee threw his hands up and yelled, "Time."

I backed off the rubber and looked to the first base side where our dugout was. I saw KB walking my way with Geno following this time. KB, Swish, and Geno all converged. This was not a check up trip. KB made his way up the mound and said, "I gotta take you out of the game."

"Are you shittin' me (a common baseball term)?"

Before I could ask why, he said, "One of the corporate lawyers with Anheiser Busch was watching the game. He made the call on the hot line to get a message down to the clubhouse to, 'Get Littell off the mound.'"

"You're shittin' me (a common baseball term)."

Geno chimed in, "In other words, if you drop dead on this very next pitch, on this Dodger mound, someone other than Anheiser-Busch could end up owning the Cardinals."

Now I'd heard it all. An f'ing lawyer was taking me out of the game; well I'll be damned. KB motioned with his left hand for Darrell Knowles to replace me on the bump. Before they could turn away I said, "Well, if I'm comin' out of the game both of you guys take an arm and let's make it look good going to the dugout."

So they each took an arm and we get to the first base line where Bill Russell asked, "Country, you all right?"

My response was, "I'm goina drill you."

At least I'd have a little bit of an upper hand the next time I faced him. It was nice to be known as conveniently wild. I always liked Bob Gibson's approach to pitching: "don't talk to the other team." I just decided to send a firm message in this case.

We got to the dugout and I headed up the runway to the clubhouse. Geno came up and said there was an ambulance waiting to take me to the hospital to get checked out.

Well sure enough, I didn't have time take off my uniform as two paramedics walked into the clubhouse lookin' for the casualty. "Here I am. Can you city boys put the pedal to the metal? Let's make this look real good, I'd love to see some showmanship."

I hopped into the middle of the ambulance and said to the driver, "Let's see what this thing can do." We headed out of the ravine kinda haulin' ass.

We made it to some hospital emergency room and they found a few of my scruples still intact. They declared me good to go.

The next day, Jack Buck, the great Cardinal broadcaster who was never at a loss for words, found me in the locker room. "Country, I wanted you to know I gave you a good plug when you charged that line drive."

Yeah, but what about that new bench coach who went by the name of "Lawyer"?

A Lawyer Takes Me Out Of A Game

PRISON TIME

Yep, I did some time at Menard Correctional Center. When I was with the Cardinals I used to step out into the community and surrounding area to make a few extra bucks and network some. You never know what's out there unless you stick your head out the door and put the pedal to the metal. The year was 1981. It was January and Marty Hendon called me to see if I wanted to go out and talk up Cardinal baseball at a sports banquet across the river in Illinois. Marty Hendon was the long-time public relations director for the St. Louis Cardinals. He was a big guy with horned rim glasses who couldn't be missed in a room. Marty knew just a plethora of information about Cardinal baseball and the St. Louis community. I was one of his go-to guys for speaking engagements, and just as long as he didn't wear me out and kept me somewhat fresh, I was game.

Marty said this talk would be at a correctional institution. All they wanted was a player to show up with a Cardinal highlights film and talk and tease 'em a little, then just come back across the river. My first question was what age these guys were.

His answer, "They're probably juvenile delinquents that just need a few good words with a little razzle-dazzle."

That sounded easy, didn't it? I asked him when and he said it would go down in about two weeks on a Friday night at 7:00 pm. Yee Haa Friday night under the lights. "Come by the stadium and I'll get you an 8MM reel film. They have a projector."

Piece of cake. What a great way to make $200. Remember, this was 1981; we weren't in the twenty first century where you had to get an O-kee-doe-kee from your agent. You did your own thing. Nor was there the minimum $2500 fee like there is now. Inflation. It was better back then, you might say. Less hassle, less government. Today we have way too much micro managing … but that's another story.

I went down on a Wednesday to Busch Stadium to make my rounds and say hi to all the folks in the office. Then I found Marty who gave me directions and the film. When I looked at the directions, I just glanced and saw Wood River, assumed it was right across from St. Louis on the Illinois side.

Really, it was fifty miles to the south (never assume, it will make an ASS-out of-U-and-ME). It cost me a quarter to make the phone call plus it took me over an hour longer to track down where Menard Correctional Center was in the state of Illinois.

My master plan was to take the scenic route at night. Must be some nice folks out there as I see a lot of familiar tractors and combines parked next to their sheds. This was corn and soybean country. Home sweet home.

Whoa hoss, I finally found a sign that said Menard Correctional Center. There wouldn't be GPS for the next twenty-five years but I had made it. Driving on a two-lane road brought back memories, and I didn't mind the drive but I did want to get there on time. I was running fifteen minutes behind but I figured these guys had some time on their hands anyway. I drove to the entrance, mulling over how this place looked damn big for a juvenile delinquent correctional institution.

It was built into the side of a bluff and right below the edge was the Mississippi river. They must really have wanted these kids to stay in at night.

I parked and grabbed the film, then walked up to the front doors. I couldn't help but notice the long string of lights reflecting off the river. I remember thinking, *"Holy shit there must be a lot of kids in this joint."* I opened the door and walked in and saw these two guard. One asked if I was Mark Littell.

"Yes sir, I made it. Got lost, but I'm here in the flesh."

They said, "Mark, we know who you are, but we have to frisk you. It's a standard procedure. We also need to look inside the film box and I need to see your driver's license."

I thought these kids must be some real bad asses. They opened the film case and I told them it was a Cardinal's highlight film. I got to the other side of the many bars and as I walked through two sets of doors they clanged shut behind me. The guards said they had let the warden know that I had made it. Now I had a question: "Are these kids I'm talking too?"

They laughed, "No, this is the Illinois State Pen for the baddest of the bad."

Oh boy.

The room was dark and grungy and somebody had forgotten to wash the windows. Why couldn't they have some of these bad boys throw some bright paint onto the walls of this very old entrance? I asked one of the guards when this place was built and he replied, "1878."

They weren't passing out much information, but let me fill you in a little bit about this prison when I had my visitation. Menard Correctional Center was a level one maximum-security adult male facility set on approximately 2,600 acres. About 41 acres were contained for inmate population where they had 6 housing units that held over 3,000 inmates. Over 50% of the inmates at one time were in for MURDER … yeah, just a walk in the park. Definitely didn't want to piss off any of these dudes. Prior to 1970, this center was name "Southern Illinois Penitentiary." Right on Marty, just a bunch a kids.

One of the better known inmates in Menard at this time was John Wayne Gacy; just a real nice guy who strangled 33 boys and young men up around Chicago. He liked to dress up as a clown to make people happy—just your normal serial killer.

The warden came down in less than two minutes and greeted me. He started filling me in on this annual sports banquet. He looked to be in his mid-forties, and wore a suit with black-rimmed glasses, dark black hair combed and doused with plenty of tonic. Pure sixties. If you'd strapped a guitar around this guy's neck and put him in a lineup with Buddy Holly and Roy Orbison, an eyewitness couldn't pick 'em apart.

On this night, they allowed some of the prisoners' spouses to come to the event. As we were walking and talking, he told me that these guys were excited about me being there, and that Cardinal baseball was primo. Most everybody had a TV in their cell.

"We have a guy that you'll meet who has knocked out everyone he's faced when the golden glove boxers come down from St. Louis. We call him 'Sudden Sam'."

We made it to the basement where the event was being held and as he opened up the door, I looked at well over a hundred inmates jammed into close quarters with a few women sprinkled into the crowd. I'll guarantee there weren't any pit bulls and paroles at this shindig. I immediately decided the warden was my best friend, who I would definitely want to keep close to all night.

I tried to get a quick lay of the land, as the prisoners were all movin' about eating and shuffling from table to table smoking cigs and bullshitting. I really didn't mind the warden staying close, and though he never stopped talking he really did have my full attention. "Yeah, we have pretty good food here. We have our own slaughter house and even raise some vegetables in the warm season."

I asked, "Are these guys alright to be around?"

"No problem, we've got plenty of guards. Plus the guys that are at this banquet are privileged. They've been on good behavior for a year and are in step with the system."

We went through the chow line and filled 'er up, then sit down at a table that had four chairs. I was thinking, *"Please just stay with me until I say my two cents and we show the film."* But sure enough, two minutes into our sit-down the warden stood up and said, "Mark I've got to talk with my assistant warden, some of these guys I'm sure really want to talk to you."

He left and immediately those three chairs were now occupied and three other guys were suddenly watching me gulp my food down. They were in their dress-for-success Sunday best pin stripes. Another inmate with stripes and a hat to match looked somewhat studious. The coke-bottle glasses were a dead giveaway. He started firing questions about next year's team. I said, "It's going to be the real deal. I feel confident we could have a real shot at winning the World Series."

One guy spoke up and said, "We love Cardinal baseball. I've got a TV and watch you guys all the time."

"Got any Cub fans in here?"

"Yep, but none at this table."

"That's good."

Another guy asked a question about Keith Hernandez, another asked about Lou Brock, another question about Bob Forshe. It was non-stop as we started to build a crowd.

"OK," I finally said. "You guys have quizzed me long enough. My turn." I looked at the first guy who had spoken up first. I was feelin' a little frisky. "Here's my question, what did you do to get into Menard?"

He looked at me and said calmly, "I'm in for murder. But it was a stray bullet, my lawyers are appealing."

Nice to know.

I looked at another inmate and he said, "Bank robbery."

The prison reporter, Scoop, said, "I was involved in some fraud but it wasn't my fault."

I'll tell you right now this was one of toughest speaking engagements I've ever encountered. When I did get up to set the tone, the crowd was unsettled after the introduction. I talked about two minutes then asked for questions, but there weren't any. I went directly to the film and then it was total darkness. I could see people squirming around and moving here and there, kinda like they were looking for popcorn but I couldn't find any. The assistant warden explained to me that this was a big night for drugs and contraband. He said the spouses would bring them in well tucked away in places where some folks really don't want to go.

The film was over, and I started chewing the fat with some of the inmates who came forward. One inmate in particular was this 6'5" stud who was put together extremely well. Right off the bat he said, "I'm an athlete. I knock out all those dudes that come down from St. Louis, they're easy." This was Sudden Sam. Great. "I want to go pro. I'm workin' out all the time."

Sam walked away as the warden came back by and said the assistant warden wanted to show me the housing units. That would be just great, a "Carte Blanche" first class tour of Menard. The warden commented, "I saw you had met Sudden Sam."

"I certainly did and he said that he wants to go pro."

"That's all fine and well but he's only got one problem, he's got another forty more years at Menard."

But, he could still practice. Time was on his side.

The assistant warden was cool. He was around thirty and had a degree in sociology. And now *he* was my new best friend. Before we went out the door to the housing units, he told me to stay close. No problem there. It was very dark at 8:30, and we had to go around a hundred feet to get to the first housing unit. He had a small flashlight with him and before we got halfway he brought up the flashlight and signaled three times to the guardhouse that was well over a hundred yards out.

"What's that for?" I asked.

"Well, if he sees silhouettes and there's no signal, the first one's over your head and if you don't stop the

second one's in you." I realized he was referring to
a bullet.

I asked him how often he changed the batteries,
and he laughed.

He opened up the door to the first housing unit
and it was just like watching a movie. The hallway
was tall and long, with a lot of cells and they were
all occupied.

"Hey Mark, I gotta go up to the second floor to
meet with an inmate, wanna go?"

"I'm right behind you."

We hustled up to the second level and walked
half way through where he met the prisoner of interest.
The prisoner was Renee, who had save money through
the prison system, and they started talking about him
getting a television for services rendered. While they
were getting down to business, I got a good look at the
home life of his cell. I'll tell you, it wasn't pretty.

I turned my attention back to Renee and noted
that she… I mean he… was dressed real pretty. Red
bikini panties, red see-through bra, and a red hose that
was wrapped around his head. I did think he could
have done a better job with the shade of lipstick he

was wearing. The assistant warden introduced me to Renee and said, "This is Mark Littell who pitches for the Cardinals."

Renee said, "I gotta get that TV, I love Cardinal baseball. Are you really Mark Littell?"

"Only if I'm throwing well," I replied.

"Renee, we have to move on, we'll work on that TV," the assistant warden said. Renee said good-bye and started moving again.

The assistant warden told me they got about .16 cents an hour, so if you didn't have connections on the outside you were null and void on the inside. Although it looked like Renee had something working on the inside. The assistant turned to me and said, "You figured that one out." Sure he was the prison poster model.

We made it back through the housing and up to the front. All of my new acquaintances saw me off around 9:30. I crossed the bridge from Chester, but not before I parked on the Missouri side and looked back across the Mississippi river at Menard Correctional Center. Like I said, Menard was backed up against a cliff, and I just thought, *no way anybody's goina get out this joint*. This excursion was one that could be carried into spring training, and made for some good talk around the clubhouse. After I told the story, we were all pulling for Renee to get the television; could always use one more Cardinal fan spreadin' the word. Marty and I had a talk as well about giving a guy a heads up the next time he went to give a speech.

Prison Time

ST. LOUIS CARDINAL BASEBALL

1982 WORLD SERIES

St. Louis and Milwaukee

There was so much talent on the '82 World Series Team. This was a firecracker of a team that was a combination of highly skilled young players and veterans who were steady and would find a way to beat you. Lonnie Smith was in left field and he carried a .307 batting average and had 9 hits into the series.

Willie McGee held down center with a .296 batting average and was a game changer, smooth as silk. "Silent" George Hendrick's arm wasn't tested much from right field, he had a steady .282 batting average and wasn't so silent at times with a long ball, he made it look easy. Ken "Obie" Oberkfell did a great job at third and continued to hit well in the series with .292 avg.

That is kind of enough said, but what speed and jumps these guys would get when the ball cleared the infield! "Praise the Lord!" My roommate Dane Iorg would fill in the blanks with timely hitting .294 avg., and he had 9 hits in the series. Tommy Herr held down second. He could cover ground to plug up holes to the right side of the field and knew just how to turn the pitcher's best friend: the double play. It was a pretty sight to watch him and Ozzie do their thing.

Ozzie Smith would become a "Hall of Famer" who was deadly in the field. He plugged up the middle. He and Whitey had their own side bet going. For every ball hit in the air, Whitey would collect. For every ball hit on the ground, Ozzie collected. Ozzie came out ahead. He also threw out a few line drives occasionally for the go ahead run.

Keith "Hondo" Hernandez was snagging everything that came his way at first base. Hondo was a hitting machine that was centered on hitting the frozen rope. He could scorch the ball and with the unfamiliar wheels of a first baseman, he would land on second base quite often. You might say Keith could be double trouble. There's a reason he won eleven gold gloves; he was an athlete and to top it off he took very well calculated chances.

The ever-steady Bob Forsch could add and subtract through the zone, 233 innings with a 15-9 record. Joaquin Andujar was one wild and crazy guy who gave 265 innings with 15-10 won loss record. That says he was also a workhorse. Steve Mura came over in a trade from San Diego and pulled his weight. John Stuper would use mental telepathy to take down the opponent. He had a good year on the bump and snagged a big win in the series. John was so cerebral that he became the long time baseball coach at Yale. These were the starters that toed the rubber every fifth day.

Lefty Dave LaPoint snagged over 150 innings while going both ways as a starter/reliever. Jim "Kitty Cat" Kaat stayed with his well put together game plan to keep hitters off balance—he too would find a way to beat you. By the way he was 43 years young at the time with 16 gold gloves to line his mantle. Veteran Doug Bair held up his side with 63 trips to the mound to hold off any surge. He was a sick puppy so he and I hit it off well. When the game was close and on the line, Whitey went to the bullpen and snagged closer Bruce Sutter, excuse me, future Hall of Famer Bruce Sutter, with his nasty ass split finger tucked in his pocket. He also won the 1982 "Cy Young Award". Bruce got that last out to push the Cardinals over the top of Milwaukee with 6-3 to win the '82' World Series.

Darrell Porter turned it up a notch and was voted NLCS and World Series most valuable player. Gene Tenace was always ready to literally tackle anything, moving or not. Then Glenn Brummer came out of nowhere and decided to steal home in the 12th against Giant's lefthander Gary Lavelle, giving the Redbirds a 5-4 win. "Brum" grew up in hog country so we traded hog and soybean stories.

These guys held the pitching staff together. When any of them stepped onto the field they didn't have to announce their presence. There were a lot of contributors along with the coaching staff that made this whole thing work. Both teams had top of the line players, that's why it went right down to the wire. Game 7 of the World Series was up for grabs. Home field advantage played into the overall scheme because if you've been around the game of baseball and ask which city has the best fans, it's a no-brainer. It's that city out in the middle of the country by the Mississippi river—St. Louis.

Whitey Herzog was the best manager I ever played for...period. He was a great communicator who stayed out of the way and let you play the game, yet, would come down your ass in a New York second if you were out of line. This was Whitey's team; we didn't have any team captains or any "rah rah" speeches, we just tried to kick ass and take prisoners.

Whitey's teams were all about chemistry and the right kind of guy. I played for him in both Kansas City and St. Louis, and I know if you crossed him there was a damn good chance you just might be gone the next day. Hell, you could be thrown into a trade to Cleveland, or end up playing with the Texas Rangers— now that was scary.

I remember when we had just lost back-to-back games around mid-season. Whitey came to the center of the clubhouse after the second loss and said, semi-jokingly, "What's wrong with you guys? Go out and mix in a steak and a beer or two. Let's kick some ass tomorrow." He walked to his office. Enough said.

Most managers would be two innings ahead in their thinking. Whitey was three if not four innings up with his cerebral mindset. It was fun to follow which direction he would go in the last three innings of a close game. He said in one of his statements in a short meeting that, "I'm already three runs up on this guy (the other manager)." We loved that kind of talk and he got a half smile out of everybody so that meant we were goina be bad boys on the field that night. In 1982, we won 92 games. That was Whitey—short, sweet, and ever so succinct.

My part in the '82 season was short-lived I only got into 16 games and would have to deal with the worst adversity I would ever face. My arm had gone strictly south and not being on the bench around the camaraderie of my teammates was the ultimate downfall. I find it funny that I still hold an all-time single season strikeout record for relievers with the Cardinals on what they call the "All Century" list. I accomplished this in '79, had a bunch of strikeouts as a closer. I just laugh when I see Lou Brock, Stan Musial, Bob Gibson, and then Mark Littell sprinkled among "Hall of Famers." All of these Cardinal records, then Country boy Littell. Go figure.

FORREST GUMP BASEBALL STATISTICS

First off, I would like to think that everybody has seen the movie *Forrest Gump*...but that's just not going to be the case. So I'll give you a quick overview: *Forrest Gump* is set in the South and is about a boy with some obstacles to overcome. Yes, he was a little off—you know, slow to catch on. When he was young, he had physical issues; he wore metal leg braces and had a crooked spine. He didn't know any better because no matter what the circumstance, his Mama was always there givin' him praise.

Well, one day he ran himself out of those braces and just kept on running. He had a gift, what we call in sport "fast twitch fiber." As he goes through life, Forrest ends up falling into some of the damnedest life-changing events that were pretty peculiar to the common human being. When at a loss for words, Mr. Gump's favorite saying was, "My momma always said, 'Life was like a box of chocolates. You never know what you're gonna get.'"

Being a bit touched in the head allowed him to be successful for the most part...in moments of stress he had no fear, he just reacted. This is more or less what I found with some of my own offset statistics. Yes, like for Forrest Gump, timing is EVERYTHING. Fortunately and unfortunately I was in the right (or wrong) place when some interesting and off-the-wall events occurred. These events are true, and make my statistics a little peculiar to most folks.

I never wore braces, but some friends and folks who have been around me might tell you, "Yeah, that boy is probably a tad off."

FIRST AND FOREMOST

St. Louis • July 2nd, 1979 1 RBI

Philadelphia • August 12th, 1981 2 RBI's

Gotta put this one first: pitchers love to hit, but when you're a closer, you don't get many chances to get into that batter's box and show what kind of damage you can really do. We feel neglected. We bunt a lot—you know, get the runner over. During my first spring training with the Cardinals, we were told to take fifty bunts in the cages before going to the showers. There were five cages set up in major league camp, and there were five very old men that dropped the ball into the pitching machine. To do this task correctly, you gotta raise up your arm with the ball in hand, and then drop the ball into the slot—the pitching machine takes care of the rest. Now, these old farts would raise their arm about fifty times per batter, and they each had to do batting practice for three of us pitchers. Hm…that's a hundred and fifty arm-raises. It must have been a hell of a workout, the way they looked—I was so very glad they didn't drop over into the machine. I loved their attire: they had the long white pants and white button-down shirts, most wore white tennis shoes, and a couple of 'em wore the V-neck no-sleeve sweater. It felt like I was walking down to the mental ward.

In 1979, Lou Brock designated himself the pitchers' bunting coach for one day. It was rare for Lou to speak up and volunteer like this, but he was true to his word even though he had first base coach Hal Lanier standing into be the fallback guy. In spite of his ever-present smirk, he taught us pretty well. His mind was probably saying, "What have I gotten myself into?"

We were a bunch of prima-donna pitchers, but he did show us the how's and why's of bunting. Yep, the Cardinal pitchers could sure as hell bunt by the time we got through spring training. We could bunt in just about any position you put us in: one knee on the ground, both knees on the ground, one hand only above the brand, behind the back (and you better be wearin' a cup). The tough one was lying on the ground and placing the one hand on the bat with the other elbow bracing you off the ground. No fear shit. Crank it up, baby.

My career in the batter's box was short, and my statistics kinda ended up loop-de-loop. I hit left and threw right, but for some stupid-ass reason, I ended up with more RBI's than hits. Two hits and three RBI's. But here's the best part: all of my RBI's came against the Phillies, and they were in different years.

In St. Louis, 1979, Tug McGraw was struggling in this one particular game, and he ended up walking me with the bases loaded— RBI number one. I couldn't believe Tug McGraw threw me four balls—glad I didn't have to swing. It was 1981 in Philadelphia, and I came up to hit with Sixto Lezcano on second and Orlando Sanchez on third. You bet I pulled the trigger and delivered. I hit the ball between first and second, just a foot off of Manny Trillo's glove, and both my Latino amigos come around to score. RBI's number two and three. My other lone hit I really can't remember, nor did I really care.

After I came back to the dugout, Whitey said that the Phillies would be asking for me in a trade. I'm just a diamond in the rough, Whitey! But really, at this time of my career, I was just mopping-up and getting bits and pieces of blown-out games. I was what you would call a "seven-run guy"—that means you "don't pitch him unless we're seven runs up or seven runs down." My arm was definitely going south.

But no shit, stats don't lie.

Mark Littell																	
Mark Littell Hitting Stats																	
Career	G	AB	R	H	2B	3B	HR	GRSL	RBI	BB	IBB	SO	SH	SF	HBP	GIDP	AVG	OBP	SLG
9 Years	316	34	1	2	0	0	0	0	3	2	0	18	1	0	0	0	.059	.111	.059

(from Baseball Almanac)

THE GOOD
St. Louis against Philly • July 1st, 1979

I won both ends of a doubleheader, which I guess not too many guys do. I ended up as a closer in the first game against Philly—I came into the top of the 8th inning with one out, the score tied at 7 apiece, and Mike Schmidt on first.

Greg Luzinski came up to hit, and ended up rolling into a double play. We then came up in the bottom of the 8th and dropped in a six spot, making it 13-7. I went back out to pitch the 9th, and picked up the win (why I pitched the 9th, I don't know). In the second game, I came into the 8th inning with 2 outs and a score of 1-1. Mike Schmidt came to the plate, but he popped the ball up to Tempy at short to get us off the field. We didn't score in the bottom of the 8th, so it was still tied up going into the 9th. "Play ball!" My defense threw some leather out there, and we got off the field with a one-two-three inning.

When we came up to hit in the bottom of the 9th, our Cardinal hitters came up clutch: Keith Hernandez got on, and Terry Kennedy drove him in for the winning run. Well holy shit, I just swooped down and snagged my second win of the day.

Most of the time, closers were used in tie ball games in their home park, unless certain circumstances, situations, or overuse presented itself— there were lots of variables. But there was a downside to this whole scenario: I had already been on the shelf for ten days because of an elbow strain. Manager Ken Boyer and pitching coach Claude Osteen just wanted to put me between the lines to see if I would need to go on the disabled list for a while. In other words, "Was there a real problem with my arm?" Well, after the second game I realized the answer was definitely, "Yes."

The reporters came flooding in, wanting to know how the arm felt after winning both ends of a double-header. "Yeah, it feels good to grab a couple wins on a Sunday afternoon. Timely hitting." I now knew what it was like to be a politician.

Longtime Cardinal pitcher Bob Forsch, a good friend, eyeballed me from a ways off. As I sat there on that stool, dodging question after question, Bob was just shaking his head and laughing. I knew what he was thinking, *"Somehow Lit just backed into a couple of timely wins, but his arm's ready to fall off."*

And it was true. I guess the vulture that swooped in and snagged my wins had noticed the fresh meat on my right arm. Of course, before leaving, the reporters had to ask: "So it looks like you're *not* going on the DL after all?"

I couldn't get around it. "Let's flip a coin on that one."

THE BAD
Visalia at Stockton, 1994

While coaching in Stockton in the California League, I had to activate myself as a pitcher. Yes, I was the pitching coach and had thrown a ton in batting practice. I had been out of the game for fourteen years, but the testosterone still oozed out...well, some. And I knew that throwing batting practice at forty-five feet was nothing like bringin' from the hill at sixty-foot-six. But on this very particular day, when we were playing the Visalia Oaks in Stockton (Visalia was the High A team for the Rockies), our manager Lamar Johnson called me into his office, greeting me with, "Bullshit."

"What's going on, Lammie?"

"Our pitcher won't be here on time to make the start. Some kind of flight problem." Our eyes met. We both knew we were out of pitching. We carried twelve, but two were aching and the rest were running on fumes.

"Why, hell, Lam. We can spread the wealth among the pitching staff. And I'll activate myself."

"You're not activating yourself—you'll get killed!"

We sat down and tried to work out some semblance of a plan, but we both knew it had about as many holes as Swiss cheese. Prayers were said under our breath—divine intervention was really our only hope. We decided to start a reliever and keep him under eighty-five pitches. Maybe we'd get six innings out of him if he didn't get his ass in a sling. After that, all we had was, "Well, this other guy can give us one, and this guy can finish up…"

Thirty minutes before game time, Lamar was still in his office, leaning back in his chair. I peeked around the corner, "Hey, Lam…come on, put my name down on the lineup card. I'll activate myself at the plate."

We went back-and-forth a little, but he finally gave in, "If you go in, I'm not responsible."

"No problem."

Naturally, we didn't tell the front office. At game time, the umpires parked their asses at home plate, waiting for each team to bring their line-up cards. In the dugout, Lamar delegated me to do the honors. Billy Hayes, manager for the Oaks, was at the plate already. I knew Billy well enough—we both lived in Phoenix, and we both had been doing this long enough to know better. I mean, everybody knew each other at this point, and we joked around after going over the ground rules. I let Billy walk away from the home plate area first. As I turned to go, I casually mentioned to the umpires, "By the way, I'm activating myself and I'm on the lineup card."

The home plate umpire looked down in surprise, "Mark…I believe you're right."

By now, each team had scanned each other's lineup cards. One time through, and you pretty much got the other side's lineup tattooed into your head. In the third inning Billy, hands on his knees and laughing, shouts at me from the third base coaching box: "You're not gonna pitch tonight, are you?"

"*I sure as hell hope not,*" thought my pea-brain. But, hey, never say never, never say always, live in the present. Still, I couldn't help thinking about Murphy's Law…anything that can go wrong will go wrong.

As it turned out, the baseball rain god decided to interfere with our master plan. Our starting pitcher was coasting through the fifth inning with two outs, when suddenly—and I've been on hundreds of baseball fields but only twice have I seen this happen—all the sprinklers shot off. Obviously, they were on a timer. My first thought was *"Rain-out!"* but I knew the ground crew would find a way to stop these pistol-pete sprinklers from doing any real damage. I guess the good part was that nobody had left and more beer was sold.

It wasn't a five-inning game yet, and to make it a game for the books you have to complete five innings of play. I got a read on the situation and told my starter to go down to the bullpen and get loose, but at around twenty-five pitches and no more than thirty minutes, he was done. At that point, I'd take him out of the game—too much cool-down and maybe he can't rebound. It was my ass more than anyone else's if a pitcher went down because I failed to look after his health. You want your manager to look good, so everybody has to be above board and ship-shape.

Things got back to normal after about twenty minutes. The umpires came out for a short meet-'n'-greet, and then it was, "PLAY BALL!" Once again, with two outs and a runner on second, Billy, our starter, took the hill. This time, Billy threw a ground ball, and we had now made it through five innings.

"Billy, you got another inning?"

"You bet."

Maybe it was going to be one of those magical nights and we'd be able to hold onto our 2-1 lead. Sure enough, Billy gave us another inning. Lamar and I knew we weren't in the clear yet, but at least there was some breathing room at this point. We now had two relievers to cover three innings. Our first reliever was a little sore, so I told Lamar that he'd be on a short leash. He took the hill in the seventh, and he stayed under twenty pitches, but Visalia took a 3-2 lead. We failed to score in the bottom of the seventh, and we took the field in the eighth with our second reliever. He was in the same boat as the last guy: short leash. He let runners on base, but we somehow managed to get out of the inning undamaged. Next inning, though, we probably wouldn't be so lucky.

I turned to Lamar and said, "We got nobody."

He said nothing.

I trotted down to the bullpen and started warming up. That 20/10 vision I once had wasn't there now, but at least I could still see the plate. Throwing batting practice at forty-five feet every day was easy, but those extra fifteen feet made it like pulling a pin and throwing a grenade. Incoming! Watch out! With two outs, I ran back to the dugout, ready to take the rubber in the top of the ninth (as ready as I'd ever be, at any rate). Our whole bullpen was in the dugout now, ready to watch the master at work—or, at least, ready to watch an old fart give up some serious line drives.

Well, holy shit, the first guy swung and tipped the ball ten inches in front of the plate! My catcher jumped up, grabbed the ball, and tagged the batter. Our bench was just roaring with that first out. The batter was stupefied. I walked the next batter, so I switched to the stretch where I used to live. The third batter topped a slow, rolling grounder to the second baseman for a force at second. Two outs. Our bench was loud—and I needed the reinforcement. I threw two pitches and got a two-hopper back to me. I barely recovered to turn and make a four-hop throw to first base for out number three. A ten-pitch inning. Yep, the bench was howling. Coming off the mound, I passed by Billy Hayes.

"Great job!" he said, laughing.

I made my way to the bench and they were going nuts—especially the pitchers. Lamar was shaking his head with that great, big, laughing grin. Yes, my arm was ready to come off. I probably topped out at seventy-two miles per hour—well below bat speed—

but, hell, I did challenge. Here was the best part: we were down 3-2 and hitting in the bottom of the ninth. Somehow, we managed to get runners on second and third with two outs. And, yes, a softly hit line drive brought 'em both in. Game winning hit delivered, we won 4-3. Littell picked up the win. Are you shittin' me? (Once again, a common baseball term.)

In 2014, I was at a SABR (Society of Baseball Research) banquet at Don & Charlie's Restaurant in Phoenix. In a nutshell, these SABR people are a lot of folks who know a lot about baseball. There were lots of baseball stories, memorabilia, and good chow. As I walked through the banquet-room door, this guy made a bee-line for me and got me cornered.

"You're Mark Littell!"

"Yes…"

"I saw you throw your last ballgame!"

I paused. Put your brain in gear, Littell. "That would have to be the Stockton game."

"Exactly," he said. "Ten pitches thrown in the ninth, Stockton gets runners on second and third, game-winner delivered with two outs."

"Yep, and my arm is still hanging," I replied.

This was the "bad" part of me activating myself. I couldn't throw batting practice for five days.

THE UGLY
St. Louis at San Francisco • May 13th and 14th, 1978

I lost three games in a twenty-four hour period. Okay, I'll call B.S. on the "twenty-four hours"—it was more like twenty-two. Yeah, this really hurt both on and off the field. I had just got my first National League win against the Dodgers on May 10th at Dodger Stadium. I threw well—struck out eight, gave up one hit, and went four and two-thirds innings. On Friday, I didn't pitch (and knew I wasn't going to), but I made the most out of trading baseballs for hotdogs. Yes, Dodger dogs are the best.

We then headed up north to San Francisco for a typical weekend series. Yes, it was colder than shit. I'm really glad Butch Yakima, our clubhouse man, threw in the football Cardinals long coats, and the big mittens were an especially nice touch. Little did I know, but May 13th and 14th, a Saturday and Sunday, were going to be pure hell.

I came into Saturday's game, and right away the Giants got two runs off me to take the lead in the seventh. They held it, and I picked up the loss. Well, shit. On Sunday, we had a doubleheader, and I came into the first game in the eighth. I gave up a run, and once again, they took the lead, held it, and I took the loss. *"Are you shittin' me?"* (A common baseball term.)

Second game of the doubleheader, and I gave up another run in the eighth. And, yes, "The Giants hold the lead!" Beyond imagination. It was either Ted Simmons or John Denny who yelled out as I was coming through our clubhouse door to get all the razors out of the locker room. Right then and there, I knew that the mound in Candlestick was straddling the San Andreas Fault and sitting dead center over Satan's den.

I never drank very much, but there was probably three times in my life that I got totally polluted. This was one of those times. I stayed in the hotel bar—the next day would be an off day in San Francisco, and I didn't want to talk to anybody.

Cardinal coaches Hal Lanier and Jack Krol saw me setting at the bar and said, "Country, wanna go out to dinner with us?"

"I'm just fine where I'm at, but thanks for the offer."

I set there and chewed the fat with just about anybody and everybody, and ended up having more than a few beverages. I'd had enough of this crap and finally wanted go to sleep. I was well polluted—hell, I was toxic. Hal and Jack checked on me after they came back from what I'm sure was a very nice dinner.

"Country, how you doing?"

"Just great, where's the mound?"

They moved on, as I proceeded to stand up. My legs wobbled as I made it off the stool, and eventually I shuffled toward the elevator. While waiting for the elevator, I chatted with a sculptured Roman dude with big nuts.

"Well, you got a pretty good set on you, buddy. That's exactly what I needed the last two days—a set like yours. Goodnight, oh studded one."

YOU'RE UP
Cleveland at Kansas City • May 21st, 1977

I was the first Royals pitcher to hit under the DH rule. Whitey Herzog wanted to keep me in the game, because we were out of pitching and we had only one regular player left on the bench.

Whitey said, "Airhead, when's the last time you hit?"

I said, "A-ball."

"Well, you're up next. I'm keeping you in the game to pitch."

Two outs, bases loaded, and I took three right down the middle from Rick Waits. I had pitched the tenth and eleventh innings, and after taking that third strike, I went out and pitched the twelfth. The Indians put up a five-spot to make the score a disgusting thirteen to seven. Any way you look at it, I just never, ever, liked pitching against, or even playing in, Cleveland. Arrest me.

RECORD BROKEN
St. Louis at Philly • August 10th, 1981

Yes, I gave up the hit to Pete Rose that gave him the National League All-Time Hit Record—3,631 is a lot of hits. I threw a fastball inside that broke his bat, but he got a hit through the 5-6 hole (between third and short). If Ozzie Smith couldn't get it, nobody gets it. Gene Tenace, a veteran with three World Series rings, was catching me, and he came out to the mound as all the hoopla started.

He lifted up his mask and said, "Way to go, big boy. You're in the f'n record books again."

*As they stopped the game for five minutes or
so, I was thinking of Stan "The Man" Musial—Hall of
Fame Cardinal, basically Mr. Baseball of St. Louis—who
was in the stands. At least we were on the road in
Philadelphia.* I felt bad because Stan was not only a
great ballplayer, but he was also a genuine kind of guy.
Another interesting statistic within Stan's 3,630 hits:
1,815 were at home and 1,815 were on the road.

Stan made it down to the field and congratulated
Rose on his accomplishment. I still felt bad.

TIMING
Cubs at St. Louis • August. 13th, 1979

In the summer of 1964, we got off the farm and
went to St. Louis to see Cardinals baseball in old
Sportsman's Park. Mom, Dad, and Eric all went—it was
about a four hour drive from the Bootheel. Our seats
were up in the nosebleed section, but I had a broken
toe from sliding into a base about a week before.
Rather than me trying to climb too many stairs, my
Dad went over to the elevator operator to ask if we
could get a ride up. Seeing that I was in a cast and on
crutches, the elevator man agreed.

As it turned out, this was also an elevator for the
Cardinal players, since their locker room was on the

second level (just like in Wrigley Field). Just as we had all gotten situated in the open-screen elevator, a ballplayer stepped in with us. I didn't know him from Adam, but my Dad knew exactly who was riding in the cage with us. He was the new guy on the Cardinals, recently traded by the Chicago Cubs.

Halfway up, my Dad said, "You're Lou Brock."

"Yes, I am."

"Glad to have you in a Cardinal uniform. Good luck!"

Lou shot back straight, "Thank you, sir."

With that, Lou stepped off the elevator and disappeared through the locker room door. I was eleven years old. We continued our ride to the top and found our seats. We could see the field real well and also see the row houses down most all streets. It was June 20th and the Cardinals were playing the San Francisco Giants. Willie Mays and company seemed to litter up the field that day as the Cards got hammered 14-3. Mom always kept score and pretty much did the play-by-play to teach and keep Eric and I glued into the game. In the 7th inning, she leaned over and said, "Well that young man you boys saw in the elevator just got his second hit." Well, that's really good Mom but the Cardinals suck right now. When the dust settled years later, I found out that the Lou Brock trade was considered the worst in Chicago Cubs history.

Flash forward fifteen years. August 13, 1979—Cardinals played the Cubs in St. Louis (now in new Busch Stadium). For over a year at this point, I had been on the Cardinal squad, alongside Lou Brock. After all this time as a Cardinal, Lou was just two hits shy of the 3,000th hit milestone. The stadium was full for two reasons: the Cardinals and Cubs were rivals and nobody wanted to miss Lou Brock getting his 3000th hit. The game got underway, and Lou led off with a hit to make it 2,999. When the fourth inning came around, he led off again, and this time he delivered a shot off pitcher Dennis Lamp's leg. Lou was now the fourteenth Major Leaguer (and the second Cardinal) to achieve 3,000 hits. They stopped the game for five minutes to let the cameras and the hoopla to do their thing.

As we moved through the game afterwards, neither side would budge. By the eighth inning, we were tied at 2-2. I came in to pitch, and the first out went for a ground ball. I walked the second batter, but to preserve the tie, I threw a 3-6-1 double-play ball—Hernandez to Templeton to Littell—to get us out of the inning. I will never forget our shortstop Gary Templeton. Tempy had a great arm and liked to show it off. When he came across second to make the first out of the double play, he decided to put a little more mustard on the ball. I was busting my ass to get to first and take the throw, but when I turned my head to pick up the ball, it was already halfway there. When the ball landed in my glove, it felt like it would take off both glove and arm—for a second, I actually didn't think I had the ball. But I looked in my glove and it was there. I flipped the ball over my shoulder like "No problem!" as it rolled to the mound.

As we were jogging in, Tempy was laughing, and said, "I had to get it there, Country!"

"No shit, Tempy."

I was probably going to have to get the pocket of my glove restrung. As you might imagine, Tempy was known for launching an occasional rocket into the first base stands.

We scored the go-ahead run in the bottom of the eighth, and I followed in the ninth with an unusually quick "one-two-three" inning, giving us the 3-2 win. Like so many times over the years, Lou had punished his old team from the North side of Chi-town once again. With all the festivities for Lou, I remembered how I had first happened to meet him in an elevator. I was an eleven-year-old then who didn't even know who he was—now I was a Cardinal myself, picking up the win as he collected his 3,000th hit. Yes, timing is everything. Crazy but true.

A HOT ONE
San Diego Padres at St. Louis • July 20th, 1978

First off, I'm sitting in the dugout watching our players take a beating. It was a 12:30, Thursday afternoon game, and the humidity and heat were off the charts. St. Louis was known to be the hottest place to play a baseball game professionally. Since I wasn't in the game, I was sippin' on water, Gatorade, anything wet, while our guys in the field were wilting at the gates of hell.

After our Wednesday night game, we had gotten a rain shower. I really didn't think about it too much then—it was a shower, it rains all the time in St. Louis. The next morning I had made it to the clubhouse a little after 9:00 am, and I crammed down a few doughnuts and whatever else was out on the spread table. I grabbed a Post-Dispatch, and as I headed over to my locker, I found out that they were still growing soybeans in the Bootheel. A few more guys trickled through the clubhouse door. I was bored. Starting at the bottom, I decided to put on my socks and stirrups, crawl into my white to-the-knee cotton undies (we hadn't heard of compression shorts) and jock, pull up the baseball pants, throw on a T-shirt, slide into my shower shoes, and then walk down to check out the field.

It was around 10:30 when I made it down to the dugout—the doughnuts had settled, and I was ready to check out what the ground crew was doing. I could see from the shower the night before that there were some wet spots on the turf with steam coming off of them. I went over to the first base line where the ground crew was hovering. It looked playable to me, but it felt kinda hot on this turf for this early in the morning.

I saw a first-class hybrid thermometer lying on the turf and said, "Hey guys, what's the temperature?"

"Well, Country Boy, right now it reads one hundred fourteen degrees."

"No shit!"

There wasn't going to be batting practice that day because it was a get-away day (road trip). You needed a little time to rebound when heading into those hot August "dog days." Today's game would test the regular everyday player—these guys would be the ones taking the real beating. At game time, it was smoking. Not too many fans were at this game (8,510), and the ones who did show were slouched down in their seats. Some were even wearing Lou's "Brockabrella"—a nice shade and cooling invention that stood taller than a cap, but it probably pissed off the guy in the seat behind you. Even for me, a seasoned Missouri boy, it was easy to see why our guys were fading away. On the floor of the dugout, from the third inning on, each player had two rectangular troughs to land in when they made it off the field. The baseball spikes we wore then had six steel cleats built into the shoe: three in the front, three in the back. After the game, most of these guys had at least three blisters on each foot. No dancing tonight.

One of the later write-ups about this game said:

One of Littell's most impressive strikeout efforts occurred on July 20 in earning the save in the Cardinals' 3-2 victory over the Padres at St. Louis. Littell got six outs, all on strikeouts. The first two batters he struck out: Ozzie Smith and Dave Winfield. [Box score].

Okay, this was written after my playing days were over. One thing not mentioned is that it ended up being 136 degrees on that polyester grass. That day on the bump drained me. I lost nine pounds in those two innings of work. I don't think anybody had enough energy left to put up a high five for the win. We made it up the runway and went straight into the clubhouse with little talk. I just lay out on the locker room floor for a good forty-five minutes after the game, spread eagle. Steve "Swish" Swisher, who caught the whole game, was probably halfway into his casket. I had a beer—an Anheuser product of course. The long shower was very nice, but we had a charter to board. We were heading to Los Angeles where we were to open up with a 7:00 game start in Chavez Ravine. It was a quiet flight out.

Eventually we would trickle into the locker room at Dodger Stadium. Every player had his own agenda when to go to the yard: some of us would catch a cab and go out early, others might take the team bus, just be on that field when batting practice started. After batting practice both teams clear off the field, but we got up front and close to a pre-game Hollywood Stars softball game. Robin Williams was the big bopper for the 'Stars', for twenty minutes we watched these guys and gals go nuts…they sure did sweat a lot for some reason. What a contrast from a day game in St. Louis with 8500 at the game verses a night game at Dodger Stadium that would pack in 52,000. Whether at home or on the road the Cardinals and the Dodgers always drew big crowds…still do. Love it.

Whether between the lines or off the lines, there's always that daily game changer of life that can keep us on the field and in the hunt. On the other hand we have to be prepared to grasp opportunity and take that confidence and poise with some moxie to get us over the humps. Those worse case scenarios are mind boggling, so be ready and well prepared with a backup plan. You can bank on making changes for those needed adjustments.

Yes siree, you can bet that every day we will be tested to see if we can hold up to our end of the deal. Like I've stated before, the question is "Can this dog hunt?" The best way to find out is to ENGAGE. When you engage you will then be given the opportunity to…

PLAY BALL

It looks like this Game will go

into 'Extra Innings' folks

so grab a cold one and

keep that seat hot!

Coming Soon....
Country Boy
Conveniently Wild

ABOUT THE AUTHOR

Mark Littell is a former professional baseball player who pitched in the Major Leagues for the Kansas City Royals and St. Louis Cardinals. He was born in Cape Girardeau but grew up in the lower Bootheel of Missouri where he started honing his baseball skills at an early age. Mark was signed by the Royals in 1971 and was on a personal fast track when he made his debut on June 14th, 1973 in Baltimore. In 1978 he was traded to the Cardinals where he finished out his career in 1982.

After leaving the MLB and down the line, Mark served as coach in-residence for Australia's

Bicentennial in 1988. He would spend three more seasons "down under." He then became a minor league pitching coach with San Diego, Milwaukee, Kansas City, and the Dodgers covering a span of 18 years. He played winter ball in Puerto Rico, coached and played in Dominican Republic, and was the speaker on the pitching phase for the Panamanian Baseball Federation.

Mark is also the inventor of the Nutty Buddy, a protective cup that won top honors from the Industrial Design Society of America. Mark remains active in the game with several club and two collegiate teams in Phoenix. He is a motivational speaker and is constantly working with players to move forward to that next level. In 2016, Mark was inducted into the Missouri Sports Hall of Fame. He currently lives in Phoenix, Arizona with his wife Sanna.

Made in the USA
Lexington, KY
08 December 2016